Privileged Access Management (PAM): From zero to hero

James Relington

DEDICATION

To all cybersecurity professionals, IT administrators, and security
enthusiasts who work tirelessly to protect digital assets and safeguard
privileged access. Your dedication to securing organizations against
ever-evolving threats inspires the continuous improvement of
Privileged Access Management. This book is dedicated to your
commitment, resilience, and passion for building a safer digital world.

AKNOWLEDGEMENTS

I would like to express my deepest gratitude to my colleagues, mentors, and industry experts who have shared their invaluable knowledge and insights on Privileged Access Management (PAM). Their guidance and expertise have been instrumental in shaping this book. I also extend my appreciation to my family and friends for their unwavering support and encouragement throughout this journey. Special thanks to the cybersecurity professionals and IT teams worldwide who work tirelessly to protect sensitive systems and data. Lastly, I am grateful to the readers of this book—your dedication to improving security practices and safeguarding digital environments is truly commendable.

Introduction to Privileged Access Management

Privileged Access Management (PAM) is a crucial security discipline that focuses on controlling, monitoring, and securing privileged accounts across an organization's IT infrastructure. These privileged accounts, which have elevated access rights, are often targeted by cybercriminals due to their ability to manipulate critical systems, access sensitive data, and execute high-impact operations. Without proper controls in place, the compromise of a single privileged account can lead to devastating consequences, including data breaches, system downtime, and regulatory non-compliance.

The need for PAM arises from the growing complexity of modern IT environments. Organizations operate in hybrid infrastructures that include on-premises servers, cloud services, and remote access points, all of which require strict access controls to mitigate risks. Traditional security measures such as firewalls and antivirus software are no longer sufficient to prevent unauthorized access, making PAM an essential component of any cybersecurity strategy. By implementing PAM, businesses can enforce strict policies on who can access privileged accounts, when, and under what conditions, thereby reducing the attack surface and minimizing security risks.

A fundamental aspect of PAM is the principle of least privilege (PoLP), which dictates that users should be granted only the minimum level of access necessary to perform their job functions. This principle helps prevent excessive permissions that could be exploited by malicious actors or abused by insiders. Enforcing least privilege through PAM ensures that even if an account is compromised, the potential damage remains limited. Organizations that fail to implement this control often struggle with privilege sprawl, where users accumulate excessive access rights over time, increasing the likelihood of security incidents.

Privileged accounts come in various forms, including administrative accounts, service accounts, and application accounts. Administrative accounts are used by IT staff to manage critical systems and perform maintenance tasks. Service accounts enable automated processes to function without manual intervention, often running background tasks essential for business operations. Application accounts facilitate communication between different software applications. Each type of privileged account carries unique risks, making it necessary to apply tailored security controls to protect them from misuse.

One of the key components of a PAM solution is a secure vault or password manager, which stores and rotates credentials for privileged accounts. Password vaulting eliminates the need for users to manually remember or share passwords, reducing the risk of credential theft. Advanced PAM solutions also incorporate multi-factor authentication (MFA) to add an extra layer of security before granting access. By requiring users to verify their identity through multiple authentication factors, such as biometrics or one-time passcodes, organizations can significantly strengthen access security.

Monitoring and auditing are integral to PAM, as they enable organizations to track privileged activities and detect suspicious behavior in real-time. PAM solutions provide session recording, which allows security teams to review actions taken within privileged sessions. This capability is essential for forensic investigations and regulatory compliance, as it helps organizations demonstrate accountability for privileged access. Continuous monitoring also enables proactive threat detection, alerting security teams to anomalies that may indicate a potential breach or insider threat.

Regulatory requirements and industry standards mandate strict controls over privileged access. Compliance frameworks such as the General Data Protection Regulation (GDPR), the Payment Card Industry Data Security Standard (PCI DSS), and the National Institute of Standards and Technology (NIST) guidelines emphasize the importance of securing privileged accounts. Organizations that fail to implement PAM risk severe penalties, reputational damage, and legal consequences. Adopting a robust PAM strategy not only helps meet compliance requirements but also enhances overall cybersecurity resilience.

Implementing PAM is not a one-time initiative but an ongoing process that requires continuous evaluation and improvement. Organizations must regularly assess their privileged access landscape, update policies, and adapt to emerging threats. Training employees on best practices for privileged access is also critical, as human error remains one of the leading causes of security breaches. A well-designed PAM program fosters a security-conscious culture and ensures that privileged access is managed effectively across all systems and applications.

As cyber threats evolve, so must the strategies for securing privileged access. PAM is no longer optional but a necessity for organizations seeking to protect their most sensitive assets. By deploying comprehensive PAM solutions, enforcing least privilege, and implementing strong authentication and monitoring mechanisms, businesses can significantly reduce the risk of privilege-related security breaches. PAM serves as a foundational pillar of modern cybersecurity, providing organizations with the control and visibility needed to safeguard critical systems and data from both external and internal threats.

The Importance of PAM in Modern Security

Privileged Access Management (PAM) is a critical component of modern cybersecurity strategies, designed to protect organizations from cyber threats that target high-level access accounts. As cyberattacks become more sophisticated and frequent, safeguarding privileged credentials is no longer optional but a necessity. Privileged accounts grant users elevated permissions to access sensitive systems, modify configurations, and manage critical business applications. If compromised, these accounts can be exploited by malicious actors to steal data, disrupt operations, and cause significant financial and reputational damage.

The increasing complexity of IT environments has made privileged access a prime target for cybercriminals. With organizations adopting hybrid infrastructures that combine on-premises systems, cloud platforms, and remote work capabilities, managing privileged access has become more challenging than ever. Traditional security approaches, which focused primarily on perimeter defense, are no longer sufficient to prevent unauthorized access. Cybersecurity strategies must now incorporate PAM solutions to mitigate risks associated with excessive privileges and prevent unauthorized access to critical systems.

One of the primary reasons PAM is essential in modern security is the role it plays in preventing insider threats. While external cyberattacks receive significant attention, insider threats—whether intentional or accidental—pose a substantial risk to organizations. Employees, contractors, and third-party vendors often require privileged access to perform their duties. However, if this access is not managed properly, it can be misused or exploited. PAM solutions enforce strict access controls, ensuring that users only have the minimum permissions required to complete their tasks. By limiting access and continuously monitoring privileged activities, organizations can reduce the risk of insider threats.

Another major advantage of PAM is its ability to mitigate the impact of credential-based attacks. Cybercriminals frequently use tactics such as phishing, brute force attacks, and credential stuffing to gain unauthorized access to privileged accounts. Once inside, they can move laterally across networks, escalating privileges and compromising additional systems. PAM solutions help prevent such attacks by enforcing strong authentication mechanisms, such as multi-factor authentication (MFA) and password rotation policies. Secure password vaults ensure that privileged credentials are stored and accessed securely, reducing the risk of unauthorized use.

Regulatory compliance is another driving factor behind the adoption of PAM. Organizations across various industries must adhere to strict regulatory standards and data protection laws, such as GDPR, PCI DSS, HIPAA, and SOX. These regulations require companies to implement strong access controls and ensure that privileged activities are logged and auditable. Failure to comply with these requirements can result in hefty fines and legal consequences. PAM solutions provide the necessary tools to enforce compliance, offering audit trails, session monitoring, and automated reporting to demonstrate adherence to regulatory frameworks.

The integration of PAM with other security technologies further enhances an organization's overall security posture. Modern PAM solutions can integrate with Security Information and Event Management (SIEM) systems, endpoint detection and response (EDR) tools, and identity and access management (IAM) platforms. These integrations allow security teams to gain real-time insights into privileged activities, detect anomalies, and respond to threats more effectively. By correlating privileged access data with other security events, organizations can improve threat detection and enhance incident response capabilities.

A well-implemented PAM strategy also supports the principle of Zero Trust security. Zero Trust operates on the assumption that no user or system should be trusted by default, regardless of whether they are inside or outside the corporate network. PAM aligns with this approach by enforcing strict verification measures and continuously monitoring privileged sessions. By implementing Just-In-Time (JIT) access, organizations can further reduce exposure by granting temporary privileged access only when necessary, instead of providing permanent administrative rights. This minimizes the attack surface and limits the potential damage of compromised accounts.

As cyber threats continue to evolve, so must security strategies. Organizations that fail to implement PAM expose themselves to significant risks, including financial losses, regulatory penalties, and reputational damage. Privileged access remains a high-value target for cybercriminals, and without robust controls in place, businesses remain vulnerable to attacks. By adopting a comprehensive PAM framework, companies can strengthen their defenses, improve compliance, and protect their most critical assets from unauthorized access. The growing reliance on digital transformation, cloud computing, and remote work only reinforces the need for a strong PAM strategy in today's security landscape.

Key Concepts and Terminology

Privileged Access Management (PAM) is built upon several core concepts and terminologies that are essential to understanding how privileged access is secured and managed within an organization. Without a clear grasp of these key terms, it becomes difficult to design and implement an effective PAM strategy. This chapter explores the fundamental concepts that form the foundation of privileged access security and the terminology commonly used in the field.

A privileged account is any user account that has elevated access rights beyond those of a standard user. These accounts can be administrative, service, or application accounts, each serving a different function within an IT environment. Administrative accounts grant users the ability to modify system settings, install software, and manage user permissions. Service accounts are used by applications and automated processes to perform system-level functions. Application accounts facilitate communication between different systems and software components, often requiring elevated privileges to function properly.

The principle of least privilege (PoLP) is a fundamental security concept in PAM. It dictates that users, applications, and systems should only be granted the minimum level of access necessary to perform their specific tasks. Implementing PoLP reduces the risk of accidental or malicious misuse of privileged accounts by limiting exposure. Organizations that fail to enforce this principle often experience privilege creep, where users accumulate excessive permissions over time, increasing the likelihood of security breaches.

A privileged session refers to any activity performed using a privileged account. These sessions must be monitored and controlled to prevent unauthorized actions and ensure accountability. Session monitoring tools allow security teams to track user activity in real-time, record privileged sessions, and analyze them for anomalies. Privileged session management (PSM) is a component of PAM that ensures all privileged sessions are securely established, monitored, and audited.

Authentication and authorization are two distinct but related concepts in PAM. Authentication verifies the identity of a user attempting to access a system, often using passwords, biometrics, or multi-factor authentication (MFA). Authorization, on the other hand, determines what actions the authenticated user is allowed to perform. A strong PAM solution integrates both authentication and authorization mechanisms to ensure that only legitimate users can access privileged accounts and perform authorized actions.

Multi-factor authentication (MFA) is a security measure that requires users to provide multiple forms of verification before gaining access to a privileged account. This typically includes something the user knows (password), something the user has (security token or mobile device), and something the user is (biometric data such as a fingerprint or facial recognition). MFA significantly enhances security by reducing the risk of credential-based attacks such as phishing and password theft.

Privileged account discovery is a critical process in PAM that involves identifying all privileged accounts within an organization. Many businesses struggle with shadow IT, where undocumented accounts exist without proper oversight, posing security risks. Automated discovery tools scan the IT environment to locate and catalog privileged accounts, ensuring that no account remains unmanaged. Once discovered, these accounts can be secured, monitored, and integrated into the PAM solution.

A password vault is a secure repository used to store and manage privileged account credentials. It enforces password policies such as complexity requirements, rotation intervals, and expiration rules. By centralizing credential storage, password vaults prevent users from relying on weak or reused passwords, reducing the likelihood of credential compromise. Advanced vaulting solutions also provide just-in-time access, where credentials are made available only when needed and expire after use.

Privileged access governance ensures that privileged accounts are granted, reviewed, and revoked in accordance with security policies and regulatory requirements. This involves regular access reviews, role-based access control (RBAC), and compliance reporting. Access reviews allow organizations to validate that users still require their privileges, while RBAC assigns permissions based on job roles rather than individual users. Compliance reporting helps organizations demonstrate adherence to security standards and industry regulations.

Threat intelligence and behavior analytics are increasingly being integrated into PAM solutions to detect and respond to suspicious activities. By analyzing patterns of user behavior, these tools can identify anomalies that may indicate a potential security threat. For example, if a privileged account suddenly attempts to access systems at unusual times or from unfamiliar locations, it can trigger an alert for further investigation.

Zero Trust Architecture (ZTA) is a modern security framework that aligns closely with PAM principles. It assumes that no user, system, or application should be automatically trusted, regardless of whether it is inside or outside the organization's network. Instead, every access request must be continuously verified based on contextual factors such as user identity, device health, and location. PAM solutions that incorporate Zero Trust principles enforce strict access controls, reducing the risk of unauthorized privileged access.

Privileged access auditing is the process of logging and reviewing all privileged activities to ensure compliance and detect potential security incidents. Audit logs provide a detailed record of who accessed privileged accounts, when, and what actions they performed. These logs are essential for forensic investigations, regulatory audits, and continuous security monitoring. Organizations that lack proper auditing mechanisms often struggle to identify the root cause of security breaches.

Understanding these key concepts and terminologies is essential for implementing an effective PAM program. By enforcing the principle of least privilege, securing privileged sessions, leveraging multi-factor authentication, and continuously monitoring privileged access, organizations can significantly reduce security risks. As cyber threats evolve, PAM remains a critical defense mechanism, ensuring that privileged accounts are properly managed and protected from exploitation.

Common Threats and Risks Without PAM

Privileged Access Management (PAM) plays a crucial role in securing an organization's critical systems and sensitive data. Without a proper PAM strategy, organizations expose themselves to a wide range of security threats that can lead to financial losses, reputational damage, and regulatory penalties. Privileged accounts, such as administrative and root accounts, have extensive access to an organization's infrastructure, making them prime targets for cybercriminals. Without PAM, these accounts can be misused, exploited, or compromised, creating severe security risks.

One of the most significant threats without PAM is credential theft. Attackers frequently use techniques such as phishing, keylogging, and brute force attacks to steal privileged credentials. Once an attacker gains access to an administrator account, they can navigate through the network, escalate privileges, and access critical systems without detection. Since privileged accounts often have broad access, a single compromised credential can lead to a complete security breach, affecting an entire organization. Without PAM, there is no structured approach to securing and rotating privileged credentials, making it easier for attackers to exploit static or weak passwords.

Lateral movement is another serious risk in the absence of PAM. Once an attacker gains initial access, they often attempt to move laterally across the network to gain control over more systems. By leveraging unsecured privileged accounts, attackers can escalate their privileges and gain administrative control over the entire IT infrastructure. Without PAM solutions to enforce least privilege access and monitor privileged sessions, organizations have little visibility into these movements, allowing attackers to operate undetected for extended periods.

Insider threats pose another major risk for organizations that do not implement PAM. Employees, contractors, and third-party vendors often require elevated privileges to perform their tasks. Without proper access controls, these users may misuse their privileges to access sensitive data, modify critical configurations, or disrupt business operations. In some cases, insiders may intentionally leak confidential information or sabotage systems for financial gain or personal motives.

Even if insider threats are not malicious, accidental misuse of privileged accounts can lead to data loss, system failures, and compliance violations. PAM helps mitigate insider risks by enforcing strict access policies, logging privileged activities, and providing audit trails for accountability.

Compliance violations are another consequence of failing to implement PAM. Many industries are governed by strict regulations, such as GDPR, HIPAA, PCI DSS, and SOX, which require organizations to protect sensitive data and enforce access controls. Without PAM, organizations may fail to meet regulatory requirements, leading to heavy fines, legal consequences, and loss of business trust. PAM solutions provide the necessary audit and reporting capabilities to demonstrate compliance, ensuring that privileged access is properly managed and documented.

The lack of session monitoring and auditing further increases security risks. Without PAM, organizations have no way of tracking who accessed privileged accounts, what actions were performed, and whether any malicious activity occurred. This lack of visibility makes it difficult to detect and respond to security incidents in real time. PAM solutions offer session recording and real-time monitoring, enabling organizations to analyze privileged activities, detect anomalies, and respond to potential threats before they escalate.

Another overlooked risk of not having PAM is the uncontrolled proliferation of privileged accounts, known as privilege sprawl. Over time, as employees change roles or systems are updated, privileged accounts tend to accumulate without proper oversight. This can result in outdated, unused, or orphaned accounts that remain active, providing an easy entry point for attackers. PAM helps prevent privilege sprawl by enabling organizations to discover, manage, and regularly review all privileged accounts, ensuring that only necessary accounts exist and are actively monitored.

Organizations without PAM also face risks associated with third-party access. Many businesses rely on external vendors, consultants, and partners who require privileged access to critical systems. Without a PAM solution to enforce temporary, time-restricted, and monitored access, these third parties can become weak links in security. If their credentials are stolen or misused, attackers can exploit their access to infiltrate the organization's infrastructure. PAM enables organizations to implement just-in-time (JIT) access, ensuring that third parties only receive the minimum privileges needed for a specific task and for a limited duration.

Ransomware and other malware attacks also become more devastating when privileged accounts are left unprotected. Attackers often use privileged credentials to disable security tools, delete backups, and spread malware across networks. Without PAM to enforce access restrictions and continuously monitor privileged sessions, organizations become highly vulnerable to widespread ransomware infections that can encrypt critical data and disrupt business operations. PAM mitigates these risks by limiting privileged access, enforcing strong authentication mechanisms, and monitoring all privileged activities for suspicious behavior.

The absence of PAM creates a security gap that exposes organizations to both external and internal threats. Cybercriminals actively seek to exploit privileged accounts due to their extensive control over critical systems. Without PAM, organizations lack the necessary controls to secure privileged credentials, monitor access, and enforce least privilege principles. By failing to implement a comprehensive PAM strategy, businesses leave themselves open to data breaches, compliance failures, and operational disruptions, all of which can have long-term consequences for their security and reputation.

The Evolution of Privileged Account Security

Privileged account security has undergone a significant transformation over the years, evolving from basic administrative controls to sophisticated, AI-driven security solutions. As organizations increasingly rely on digital infrastructures, the need to secure privileged access has become a critical priority. The evolution of privileged account security reflects the growing complexity of IT environments, the rise of cyber threats, and the shift toward compliance-driven security models.

In the early days of computing, privileged access was primarily managed through simple administrative accounts. IT administrators had unrestricted access to systems, often using shared credentials that remained unchanged for years. Security measures were minimal, as the primary concern was operational efficiency rather than cybersecurity. At that time, threats were relatively limited, with most risks stemming from accidental misconfigurations or insider misuse rather than external cyberattacks.

As networked computing and the internet became more prevalent, the security landscape changed dramatically. Organizations began connecting their internal systems to external networks, increasing the risk of unauthorized access. Cybercriminals started exploiting weak administrative controls, using tactics such as password guessing and brute force attacks to gain access to privileged accounts. The realization that privileged credentials were a prime target led to the first generation of privileged access controls, which included stronger password policies and user authentication mechanisms.

The rise of regulatory compliance further accelerated the need for better privileged account security. Regulations such as Sarbanes-Oxley (SOX), HIPAA, and PCI DSS introduced strict requirements for access control and auditing. Organizations were required to implement logging mechanisms to track who accessed privileged accounts and what actions were performed. This shift marked the beginning of a more structured approach to privileged access management, focusing on visibility, accountability, and compliance.

The introduction of password vaulting solutions represented a major milestone in privileged account security. Instead of relying on static passwords, organizations began using password vaults to securely store and rotate credentials. This eliminated the risk of users manually managing privileged passwords, reducing the likelihood of credential theft. Additionally, multi-factor authentication (MFA) became a standard requirement, adding an extra layer of security to privileged access.

With the expansion of cloud computing and remote work, privileged account security faced new challenges. Traditional perimeter-based security models were no longer sufficient, as employees and third-party vendors required access to critical systems from various locations. The Zero Trust security model emerged as a response to these challenges, emphasizing the need to verify every access request regardless of the user's location. Privileged Access Management (PAM) solutions evolved to support Just-In-Time (JIT) access, granting users temporary privileges only when needed, further reducing the attack surface.

Automation and artificial intelligence (AI) have played a key role in the most recent advancements in privileged account security. AI-driven analytics now enable real-time detection of anomalous behavior, allowing organizations to identify and respond to potential threats before they escalate. Behavioral analytics help differentiate normal user activity from suspicious actions, reducing false positives while improving overall security posture.

The future of privileged account security continues to evolve as organizations adopt emerging technologies such as identity-based access controls, cloud-native PAM solutions, and AI-driven threat intelligence. As cyber threats become more sophisticated, the emphasis on proactive security measures, continuous monitoring, and automated response will continue to shape the evolution of privileged access management. Organizations that fail to adapt to these advancements risk falling behind, exposing themselves to significant security threats and compliance challenges.

Standards and Frameworks for PAM

Privileged Access Management (PAM) is an essential component of modern cybersecurity, ensuring that critical systems and sensitive data remain secure from unauthorized access. To establish effective PAM policies, organizations must align with widely recognized standards and frameworks that provide best practices for managing privileged accounts. These standards serve as guidelines for implementing security controls, ensuring compliance with regulations, and mitigating risks associated with privileged access.

One of the most widely adopted security frameworks for PAM is the National Institute of Standards and Technology (NIST) Cybersecurity Framework. NIST provides a structured approach to managing cybersecurity risks, emphasizing the need to identify, protect, detect, respond to, and recover from security threats. In the context of PAM, NIST recommends enforcing strict authentication mechanisms, continuously monitoring privileged access, and implementing least privilege principles to reduce the attack surface. Organizations that follow NIST guidelines enhance their security posture by ensuring that privileged accounts are properly managed and monitored.

Another critical standard is the ISO/IEC 27001, an internationally recognized framework for information security management systems (ISMS). This standard outlines best practices for securing information assets, including privileged accounts. ISO 27001 requires organizations to implement role-based access control (RBAC), enforce strong authentication, and maintain detailed logs of privileged activities. Compliance with ISO 27001 helps organizations demonstrate their commitment to cybersecurity and provides a structured approach to managing privileged access risks.

The Payment Card Industry Data Security Standard (PCI DSS) is particularly relevant for organizations that handle payment transactions. This standard mandates strict controls over privileged access to cardholder data environments. PCI DSS requires organizations to enforce multi-factor authentication (MFA) for administrative access, implement password vaulting solutions, and monitor privileged account activity. Failure to comply with PCI DSS can result in financial penalties, legal consequences, and reputational damage.

For organizations operating in highly regulated industries, the Sarbanes-Oxley Act (SOX) establishes requirements for securing financial data and preventing fraud. PAM plays a crucial role in SOX compliance by ensuring that only authorized users can access sensitive financial systems. Organizations must implement access controls, maintain audit trails, and regularly review privileged account usage to prevent unauthorized modifications to financial records. By adhering to SOX guidelines, businesses can enhance their financial security and reduce the risk of fraud.

The General Data Protection Regulation (GDPR) also emphasizes the importance of managing privileged access, particularly when handling personal data of EU citizens. GDPR requires organizations to implement security measures that protect sensitive information from unauthorized access. PAM solutions that enforce least privilege access, monitor privileged sessions, and ensure accountability through detailed logs help organizations meet GDPR requirements. Non-compliance with GDPR can lead to severe penalties, making privileged access security a top priority for businesses handling personal data.

The Center for Internet Security (CIS) Critical Security Controls provides a comprehensive set of security best practices, including specific guidelines for managing privileged accounts. The CIS framework recommends enforcing just-in-time (JIT) access, implementing strong authentication measures, and continuously auditing privileged activities. Organizations that follow CIS recommendations can effectively reduce the risk of privilege-related security breaches and strengthen their overall cybersecurity defenses.

Another relevant framework is the Federal Risk and Authorization Management Program (FedRAMP), which applies to cloud service providers working with U.S. federal agencies. FedRAMP establishes stringent security requirements, including robust privileged access controls. Cloud providers must implement PAM solutions that secure privileged credentials, enforce access restrictions, and ensure continuous monitoring of privileged sessions. Adhering to FedRAMP guidelines enables cloud providers to meet federal security requirements while protecting government data.

The Cybersecurity Maturity Model Certification (CMMC) is another framework that emphasizes privileged access security, particularly for organizations working with the U.S. Department of Defense. CMMC includes specific controls for managing privileged access, such as enforcing least privilege, implementing session monitoring, and ensuring continuous assessment of privileged account security.

Organizations seeking to work with the Department of Defense must demonstrate compliance with CMMC to ensure they meet stringent security requirements.

As cyber threats evolve, adherence to these standards and frameworks is essential for securing privileged access and maintaining regulatory compliance. By aligning PAM strategies with industry best practices, organizations can establish strong access controls, minimize security risks, and protect their most critical assets from cyber threats.

Building a PAM Strategy

Developing a comprehensive Privileged Access Management (PAM) strategy is essential for securing an organization's most critical assets and reducing the risk of security breaches. As privileged accounts hold the keys to sensitive systems and data, a well-structured PAM approach ensures that access is controlled, monitored, and audited. Without a clear strategy, organizations face significant risks, including credential theft, unauthorized access, and compliance violations. A strong PAM strategy is built upon key principles such as least privilege, continuous monitoring, and automation to enhance security while maintaining operational efficiency.

The foundation of a PAM strategy begins with privileged account discovery. Organizations must first identify all privileged accounts across their IT environment, including administrative accounts, service accounts, application accounts, and third-party access credentials. Many organizations struggle with privilege sprawl, where privileged accounts accumulate over time without proper oversight. An automated discovery process helps locate all privileged accounts, ensuring that none remain unmanaged or unprotected. Once identified, these accounts must be categorized based on their access levels, criticality, and associated risks.

Defining access policies is a crucial next step in building a PAM strategy. Organizations should implement the principle of least privilege (PoLP), ensuring that users receive only the minimum access necessary to perform their job functions. Role-based access control (RBAC) and just-in-time (JIT) access provisioning further strengthen security by restricting access based on predefined roles and granting temporary privileges only when required. These policies should be reviewed regularly to adapt to changing business needs and security threats.

Credential management is another fundamental component of PAM. Privileged passwords should never be shared or stored in unsecured locations. A centralized password vault allows organizations to securely store, rotate, and enforce strong password policies for privileged accounts. Automated password rotation ensures that credentials are frequently changed, reducing the risk of unauthorized access due to stolen or leaked passwords. Additionally, multi-factor authentication (MFA) should be mandated for all privileged access, adding an extra layer of security beyond traditional passwords.

Session management and monitoring play a critical role in detecting and preventing misuse of privileged accounts. Organizations should implement session recording and real-time monitoring to track all privileged activities. Privileged session management (PSM) tools provide visibility into user actions, allowing security teams to detect anomalies, investigate suspicious behavior, and enforce security policies. Recorded sessions also serve as valuable audit logs, supporting forensic investigations and compliance reporting.

PAM should be integrated with existing security frameworks, including identity and access management (IAM) systems, security information and event management (SIEM) solutions, and endpoint protection platforms. These integrations help organizations gain a holistic view of their security posture, correlate privileged access data with broader threat intelligence, and automate incident response workflows. When an anomaly is detected, automated threat response mechanisms can restrict or revoke privileged access to contain potential security incidents.

Training and awareness are essential for the success of any PAM strategy. Employees, administrators, and third-party vendors must understand the importance of privileged access security and follow best practices for handling privileged credentials. Regular security awareness training ensures that users remain vigilant against social engineering attacks, phishing attempts, and improper access practices. Organizations should also establish clear policies for requesting, approving, and revoking privileged access to maintain accountability.

Compliance and audit readiness are additional considerations when building a PAM strategy. Regulatory frameworks such as GDPR, PCI DSS, HIPAA, and NIST require organizations to enforce strict privileged access controls and maintain detailed audit logs. PAM solutions provide automated reporting and compliance dashboards, helping organizations demonstrate their adherence to regulatory requirements. Regular internal audits and access reviews ensure that privileged access remains aligned with security policies and industry standards.

An effective PAM strategy is not a one-time implementation but an ongoing process that requires continuous improvement. As organizations expand their digital footprint, adopt cloud-based environments, and integrate new technologies, PAM policies must evolve to address emerging threats. Regular risk assessments, policy updates, and security enhancements help organizations stay ahead of attackers and maintain a strong security posture. By leveraging automation, AI-driven analytics, and best practices, organizations can build a resilient PAM strategy that minimizes risk while enabling secure and efficient privileged access management.

Assessing Your Privileged Account Landscape

Understanding and evaluating the privileged account landscape within an organization is a fundamental step in establishing a strong Privileged Access Management (PAM) strategy. Without a comprehensive assessment, organizations face the risk of unmanaged privileged accounts, excessive access rights, and potential security vulnerabilities. Proper assessment allows for identifying risks, implementing necessary controls, and ensuring compliance with security policies and regulatory requirements.

The first step in assessing privileged accounts is identifying all accounts that have elevated access across the organization. This includes administrative accounts, service accounts, application accounts, and accounts with elevated privileges in cloud environments. Many organizations struggle with privilege sprawl, where accounts accumulate excessive access over time without proper oversight. Conducting an account discovery process using automated tools helps organizations locate all privileged accounts, ensuring none remain unmanaged.

Once privileged accounts are identified, the next step is to analyze their usage patterns and access levels. Not all privileged accounts require the same level of access, and organizations must categorize accounts based on their function and sensitivity. Accounts that provide access to critical systems, databases, or infrastructure should be prioritized for enhanced security controls, such as multi-factor authentication (MFA), session monitoring, and strict password policies.

An essential part of assessing the privileged account landscape is understanding the lifecycle of privileged access. Organizations must define how privileged accounts are created, assigned, used, and decommissioned. Without proper governance, accounts may remain active long after they are needed, increasing the risk of unauthorized access. Implementing a structured approach to privileged account management ensures that accounts are only available for legitimate use and are revoked when no longer necessary.

Assessing privileged accounts also involves reviewing existing access policies and controls. Organizations should evaluate whether their current policies enforce the principle of least privilege, ensuring that users and applications have only the minimum permissions required to perform their tasks. If excessive permissions are identified, organizations should take immediate action to limit access and enforce stricter role-based access control (RBAC) policies.

Monitoring and auditing privileged access is a critical aspect of the assessment process. Organizations should implement logging and session recording to track privileged account activities. Regular audits help detect unauthorized access attempts, privilege abuse, and potential security threats. Automated alerts and anomaly detection mechanisms enhance security by notifying security teams of suspicious activities, allowing for immediate response and mitigation.

Third-party access must also be assessed when evaluating privileged accounts. Many organizations grant privileged access to external vendors, contractors, and partners, increasing the risk of security breaches. Implementing just-in-time (JIT) access and temporary privilege escalation mechanisms ensures that third-party users only receive access for a limited time and for specific tasks, reducing the risk of persistent privileged access.

A comprehensive privileged account assessment should also include a review of password management practices. Weak, shared, or static passwords pose a significant security risk. Organizations should implement automated password rotation, enforce strong password policies, and utilize secure vaulting solutions to store privileged credentials. These measures help prevent credential theft and unauthorized access to privileged accounts.

Regular assessments of the privileged account landscape should be an ongoing practice rather than a one-time activity. Cyber threats continue to evolve, and organizations must adapt their PAM strategies accordingly. By continuously evaluating privileged accounts, enforcing access controls, and monitoring privileged activities, organizations can strengthen their overall security posture and minimize the risk of privilege-related security breaches.

Privileged Account Discovery and Inventory

Identifying and managing privileged accounts is a crucial first step in implementing a robust Privileged Access Management (PAM) strategy. Many organizations struggle with hidden or unmanaged privileged accounts, which can create security blind spots and increase the risk of unauthorized access. Privileged Account Discovery and Inventory is the process of locating, cataloging, and assessing all privileged accounts across an organization's IT environment to ensure they are properly secured and monitored.

Privileged accounts exist in various forms, including administrative accounts, service accounts, application accounts, and domain accounts. These accounts often have elevated permissions that allow users or systems to modify configurations, access sensitive data, or control critical infrastructure. Without proper discovery and inventory management, these accounts can become a significant security risk if left unchecked or if credentials are compromised.

The first step in privileged account discovery is scanning the IT environment to identify all existing privileged accounts. This process should include on-premises systems, cloud environments, databases, and network devices. Automated discovery tools help organizations detect accounts that may have been forgotten, abandoned, or created without proper oversight. These tools can analyze Active Directory, cloud platforms, and other systems to generate a comprehensive list of privileged accounts.

Once privileged accounts are discovered, organizations must classify them based on their level of access, usage patterns, and security risks. High-risk accounts, such as domain administrators or root accounts, require stricter controls and monitoring compared to lower-privileged service accounts. By categorizing accounts, security teams can prioritize risk mitigation efforts and implement appropriate access controls.

An effective inventory process also involves tracking account ownership and lifecycle management. Organizations must assign clear ownership to each privileged account to ensure accountability. Additionally, regular audits should be conducted to review access privileges and identify any accounts that are no longer needed. Orphaned accounts—privileged accounts that are no longer associated with an active employee or system—pose a significant security risk and should be disabled or removed immediately.

Privileged account inventory should be continuously updated to reflect changes in the IT environment. As employees change roles, applications are decommissioned, or new systems are introduced, privileged access requirements evolve. Keeping an up-to-date inventory ensures that organizations maintain visibility into who has privileged access and whether it aligns with security policies.

Another critical aspect of privileged account discovery and inventory is enforcing password management policies. Many privileged accounts rely on static passwords that, if left unchanged for extended periods, become susceptible to credential theft. A centralized PAM solution can integrate with privileged account inventories to enforce password rotation, multi-factor authentication (MFA), and access approval workflows.

Privileged account discovery and inventory also play a key role in regulatory compliance. Standards such as GDPR, PCI DSS, and ISO 27001 require organizations to have visibility into privileged access and enforce strong access controls. By maintaining an accurate inventory of privileged accounts, organizations can demonstrate compliance with industry regulations and reduce the risk of security violations.

By proactively discovering, categorizing, and managing privileged accounts, organizations can reduce the attack surface and strengthen their overall security posture. A well-maintained privileged account inventory provides the foundation for effective PAM implementation, ensuring that privileged access is controlled, monitored, and aligned with business security requirements.

Understanding Access Levels and Roles

Privileged Access Management (PAM) relies on a structured approach to access control, ensuring that users and systems receive only the permissions necessary to perform their designated tasks. A fundamental aspect of PAM is the classification of access levels and the assignment of roles, which help organizations enforce security best practices while maintaining operational efficiency. Without clear definitions of access levels and roles, organizations risk excessive privilege distribution, unauthorized access, and increased exposure to security threats.

Access levels define the degree of control a user or system has over resources, applications, and data. At the most basic level, organizations typically classify access into three main categories: standard users, privileged users, and administrative users. Standard users have minimal permissions, allowing them to perform basic tasks without modifying critical settings. Privileged users, such as IT support staff or application managers, have higher-level access to perform maintenance or troubleshooting. Administrative users, often referred to as superusers or domain administrators, have the highest level of control, enabling them to configure systems, manage user accounts, and override security settings.

Roles provide a structured way to assign access privileges based on job functions rather than individual users. Role-Based Access Control (RBAC) is a widely used methodology in PAM that ensures users receive only the permissions needed for their specific roles. For example, a database administrator (DBA) role may have permissions to modify database schemas and manage backups, while a finance role may have access to financial records without the ability to alter system configurations. Defining roles prevents privilege creep, where users accumulate excessive permissions over time due to changes in responsibilities.

Organizations can further refine access control using Attribute-Based Access Control (ABAC), which incorporates additional parameters such as location, device type, or time of access. ABAC enhances security by enforcing dynamic policies, ensuring that access is granted only under specific conditions. For instance, a privileged user may be allowed to access a system only from a corporate network during business hours but denied access from an external location.

Another critical aspect of access management is the principle of least privilege (PoLP), which dictates that users and systems should be granted the minimum level of access required to complete their tasks. Enforcing PoLP reduces the risk of privilege misuse, whether from malicious insiders, external attackers, or accidental actions. PAM solutions support PoLP by enabling just-in-time (JIT) access, which provides temporary elevated privileges only when necessary and revokes them after use.

Segregation of duties (SoD) is another key control mechanism that prevents conflicts of interest and reduces fraud risks. SoD ensures that no single user has control over multiple critical processes. For example, an employee responsible for processing payments should not also have the authority to approve those payments. By enforcing SoD through well-defined access roles, organizations can prevent unauthorized activities and enhance accountability.

Monitoring and auditing access levels and roles is essential to maintaining security over time. Regular access reviews help organizations identify excessive or outdated privileges, ensuring that roles align with current business needs. Automated auditing tools can track privilege changes, detect anomalies, and generate compliance reports for regulatory requirements. By continuously monitoring access assignments and refining role definitions, organizations strengthen their security posture and minimize risks associated with privilege abuse.

Understanding access levels and roles is fundamental to a secure PAM strategy. By implementing structured role-based access controls, enforcing least privilege, and regularly reviewing access assignments, organizations can effectively manage privileged access, reduce security risks, and maintain compliance with industry standards.

Developing a Privileged Access Policy

A Privileged Access Policy serves as the foundation for managing and securing privileged accounts within an organization. It establishes guidelines, rules, and best practices to ensure that privileged access is granted, monitored, and revoked in a structured and secure manner. Without a well-defined policy, organizations risk unauthorized access, privilege misuse, and compliance violations, leaving critical systems vulnerable to cyber threats.

The first step in developing a privileged access policy is identifying the scope of privileged access. Organizations must determine which accounts, systems, and applications require elevated permissions. Privileged accounts may include IT administrators, service accounts, application accounts, and third-party access credentials. By defining the scope, organizations can ensure that all privileged accounts are covered by security controls and are not left unmanaged.

Defining roles and responsibilities is another essential aspect of a privileged access policy. Organizations must establish who is responsible for granting, reviewing, and revoking privileged access. Typically, security teams, IT administrators, and compliance officers work together to enforce access controls. Assigning clear ownership of privileged accounts ensures accountability and prevents unauthorized privilege escalation.

Access control principles, such as the Principle of Least Privilege (PoLP) and Segregation of Duties (SoD), should be integrated into the policy. The PoLP ensures that users receive only the minimum access necessary to perform their tasks, reducing the risk of privilege abuse. SoD prevents conflicts of interest by ensuring that no single user has excessive control over critical processes, such as approving and executing financial transactions.

Authentication requirements should be clearly defined within the policy. Strong authentication mechanisms, such as multi-factor authentication (MFA), should be enforced for all privileged accounts. Implementing MFA adds an extra layer of security, making it significantly harder for attackers to compromise privileged credentials through phishing or credential-stuffing attacks.

The policy should also include guidelines for privileged session management. Organizations must establish procedures for monitoring, recording, and auditing privileged sessions to detect suspicious activities. Privileged session monitoring tools help security teams track user actions in real time, providing valuable insights into potential security threats and ensuring compliance with industry regulations.

Another critical component of the privileged access policy is credential management. Organizations should mandate the use of secure password vaults, automated password rotation, and strong password policies to prevent credential misuse. Static or shared passwords should be eliminated in favor of dynamic, frequently rotated credentials managed by PAM solutions.

Regular access reviews and audits should be incorporated into the policy to ensure that privileged accounts are appropriately managed over time. Periodic access reviews help identify inactive or unnecessary accounts, allowing organizations to revoke unnecessary privileges and minimize security risks. Automated auditing and reporting capabilities streamline this process, ensuring continuous compliance with security standards.

A well-defined privileged access policy must also address third-party access management. Vendors, contractors, and external partners often require temporary privileged access to critical systems. The policy should enforce strict approval workflows, just-in-time (JIT) access provisioning, and continuous monitoring of third-party privileged sessions. Implementing time-based access restrictions ensures that third parties only have access when necessary, reducing security exposure.

Incident response and breach containment procedures should be clearly outlined in the policy. In the event of a compromised privileged account, organizations must have predefined protocols for revoking access, conducting forensic investigations, and mitigating further risks. Automated threat detection mechanisms can help identify anomalies and trigger immediate response actions to minimize the impact of security breaches.

Developing a privileged access policy is not a one-time effort but an ongoing process. As cyber threats evolve and regulatory requirements change, organizations must continuously update and refine their policies. Regular policy reviews, employee training, and PAM technology enhancements ensure that privileged access remains secure and aligned with business and security objectives. By implementing a comprehensive privileged access policy, organizations can protect their most critical assets while maintaining compliance and reducing the risk of privilege-related cyber threats.

Access Approval and Governance

Access approval and governance are critical components of Privileged Access Management (PAM), ensuring that privileged access is granted based on security policies, business needs, and compliance requirements. Without structured approval workflows and governance mechanisms, organizations risk unauthorized access, privilege abuse, and regulatory violations, all of which can lead to security breaches and operational disruptions.

The access approval process begins with defining clear criteria for granting privileged access. Organizations must establish role-based access controls (RBAC) to ensure that users receive only the permissions necessary for their job functions. This prevents privilege creep, where users accumulate excessive access rights over time, increasing the risk of insider threats and unauthorized actions. Just-In-Time (JIT) access models further enhance security by granting temporary elevated privileges only when needed and automatically revoking them after use.

A formalized request and approval workflow is essential to ensure that privileged access is granted based on legitimate business needs. Access requests should go through multiple levels of review, typically involving the requestor's manager, IT administrators, and security teams. Automated PAM solutions facilitate this process by enforcing predefined approval policies, tracking requests, and maintaining an audit trail of access decisions.

Governance in PAM extends beyond initial access approvals to continuous oversight of privileged accounts. Regular access reviews help organizations identify unnecessary privileges, inactive accounts, and potential security risks. Periodic certifications, where managers and security teams revalidate user privileges, ensure that access remains appropriate over time. These reviews also support compliance with regulations such as GDPR, SOX, and PCI DSS, which mandate strict access controls and auditing.

Privileged session monitoring and auditing are key governance practices that enhance visibility into privileged activities. Organizations should implement session recording and real-time monitoring to track user actions, detect suspicious behavior, and prevent misuse of elevated privileges. Logging all privileged activities allows security teams to conduct forensic investigations, ensuring accountability and compliance with industry standards.

Third-party access governance is another critical aspect of privileged access management. Vendors, contractors, and partners often require temporary privileged access to perform specific tasks. Organizations must enforce strict approval workflows, enforce time-limited access, and continuously monitor third-party privileged activities to reduce security exposure.

Incident response procedures should also be integrated into access governance frameworks. In cases of privilege misuse or a suspected security breach, organizations must have predefined protocols for revoking access, investigating anomalies, and mitigating risks. Automated threat detection mechanisms in PAM solutions can identify abnormal privileged behavior and trigger immediate security actions.

Effective access approval and governance require a combination of policy enforcement, automation, and continuous monitoring. By implementing structured approval workflows, conducting regular access reviews, and integrating privileged session monitoring, organizations can maintain a secure and compliant privileged access environment. These practices help minimize the risks associated with privileged accounts while ensuring that business operations remain efficient and secure.

Implementing Least Privilege Principles

The Principle of Least Privilege (PoLP) is a foundational security concept that ensures users, applications, and systems are granted only the minimum access necessary to perform their tasks. By restricting privileges, organizations reduce the risk of unauthorized access, privilege abuse, and security breaches. Implementing least privilege is a critical component of Privileged Access Management (PAM) and helps strengthen an organization's overall cybersecurity posture.

The first step in implementing least privilege is conducting a comprehensive assessment of existing access rights. Organizations must review all user accounts, applications, and systems to determine their current privilege levels. Many organizations suffer from privilege creep, where users accumulate excessive permissions over time. A thorough audit helps identify overprivileged accounts and provides a basis for enforcing least privilege policies.

Once privileges are assessed, organizations should implement Role-Based Access Control (RBAC) to standardize permissions based on job roles. Instead of granting individual users custom privileges, RBAC assigns access rights according to predefined roles. For example, a help desk technician may have permission to reset passwords but not modify system configurations. By implementing RBAC, organizations ensure that access is granted based on business needs rather than individual requests.

Just-In-Time (JIT) access is another effective strategy for enforcing least privilege. Instead of providing permanent administrative privileges, JIT access allows users to request elevated permissions only when needed and for a limited duration. Temporary access reduces the window of opportunity for attackers to exploit privileged credentials. Automated PAM solutions can facilitate JIT access by provisioning and revoking privileges dynamically based on approval workflows.

Application and service accounts must also adhere to least privilege principles. Many applications run with excessive permissions by default, increasing the risk of exploitation. Organizations should review and restrict service account permissions, ensuring they have only the access required for their specific functions. Implementing credential management solutions, such as password vaulting and automated rotation, further reduces the risk of credential misuse.

Multi-Factor Authentication (MFA) should be enforced for all privileged accounts to prevent unauthorized access. Even if an attacker obtains a user's credentials, MFA adds an additional layer of security, requiring a second form of authentication, such as a mobile token or biometric verification.

Monitoring and auditing privileged access is essential for maintaining least privilege. Organizations should implement real-time logging and session recording to track privileged activities. If an account exhibits unusual behavior, such as accessing sensitive systems outside normal working hours, security teams can investigate and take action. Automated anomaly detection tools further enhance security by identifying potential privilege abuse.

Regular access reviews ensure that privileges remain aligned with business needs. As employees change roles or leave the organization, their access rights should be adjusted accordingly. Automated PAM solutions can streamline access review processes by providing detailed reports on privilege assignments and usage patterns.

By implementing least privilege principles, organizations minimize security risks while maintaining operational efficiency. Enforcing least privilege through RBAC, JIT access, credential management, and continuous monitoring ensures that users and systems only have the access necessary to perform their duties. This proactive approach strengthens cybersecurity defenses, reduces insider threats, and enhances regulatory compliance.

Authentication Mechanisms for Privileged Accounts

Authentication is a critical component of Privileged Access Management (PAM), ensuring that only authorized users can access privileged accounts. Given the high level of access these accounts provide, strong authentication mechanisms are necessary to protect them from unauthorized use, credential theft, and cyberattacks. Organizations must implement robust authentication controls to verify the identity of users before granting access to sensitive systems and administrative privileges.

The foundation of authentication for privileged accounts begins with password security. While passwords remain a primary authentication method, relying solely on them poses significant security risks. Weak, reused, or easily guessable passwords make privileged accounts vulnerable to brute force attacks, phishing, and credential stuffing. To mitigate these risks, organizations must enforce strict password policies, including complex password requirements, periodic rotation, and secure storage using password vaults.

Multi-Factor Authentication (MFA) is a crucial enhancement to password-based authentication. MFA requires users to provide additional verification factors beyond just a password. These factors typically fall into three categories: something the user knows (password or PIN), something the user has (security token or mobile authenticator), and something the user is (biometric verification such as fingerprint or facial recognition). Implementing MFA for privileged accounts significantly reduces the risk of unauthorized access, even if credentials are compromised.

Another important authentication mechanism is Public Key Infrastructure (PKI)-based authentication. PKI uses digital certificates and cryptographic key pairs to authenticate users securely. Instead of relying on passwords, users authenticate with a private key stored on a secure device, such as a smart card or hardware security module (HSM). This method ensures strong authentication while eliminating the risks associated with password-based authentication.

Single Sign-On (SSO) solutions streamline authentication for privileged users by allowing them to access multiple systems with a single set of credentials. While SSO enhances usability and reduces password fatigue, it must be implemented alongside strong authentication controls to prevent unauthorized access if an SSO session is compromised. Integrating SSO with MFA adds an extra layer of protection.

Just-In-Time (JIT) authentication further enhances security by granting privileged access only when needed. Instead of maintaining permanent administrator accounts, JIT authentication provisions temporary access credentials that expire after a specified duration. This minimizes the attack surface and ensures that privileged accounts are not constantly exposed to potential threats.

Behavioral-based authentication is an advanced mechanism that uses machine learning to analyze user behavior and detect anomalies. If a privileged account exhibits unusual activity, such as login attempts from an unfamiliar location or device, access can be restricted or require additional verification. This adaptive authentication approach enhances security by identifying and mitigating potential threats in real time.

Privileged access authentication should be continuously monitored and logged. Organizations must implement audit trails to track authentication attempts, detect failed login attempts, and identify suspicious access patterns. Centralized logging and integration with Security Information and Event Management (SIEM) solutions help security teams analyze authentication events and respond to potential security incidents promptly.

Strong authentication mechanisms are essential for securing privileged accounts against cyber threats. By implementing MFA, PKI, JIT access, and behavioral-based authentication, organizations can significantly enhance security while maintaining usability. Continuous monitoring and logging further strengthen authentication processes, ensuring that privileged access remains protected from unauthorized use and cyberattacks.

Multi-Factor Authentication (MFA) for PAM

Multi-Factor Authentication (MFA) is a fundamental security control in Privileged Access Management (PAM), designed to enhance the authentication process and protect privileged accounts from unauthorized access. Given the critical nature of privileged accounts, which grant users elevated access to sensitive systems and data, traditional password-based authentication is no longer sufficient. Cyber threats such as phishing, credential stuffing, and brute force attacks have made it essential for organizations to adopt stronger authentication measures. MFA significantly reduces the risk of compromised credentials by requiring multiple verification factors before granting access.

The core principle of MFA is that authentication should rely on at least two or more independent factors. These factors fall into three primary categories: something the user knows, such as a password or PIN; something the user has, such as a smart card, hardware token, or mobile authentication app; and something the user is, such as biometric data like fingerprints or facial recognition. By combining multiple authentication factors, MFA ensures that even if one factor is compromised, an attacker cannot gain access without the additional verification steps.

Implementing MFA within a PAM framework strengthens security by ensuring that privileged users undergo a rigorous authentication process before accessing high-risk systems. Privileged accounts are often targeted by attackers because they provide broad administrative control. If an attacker gains access to a privileged account without additional authentication layers, they can move laterally through an organization's infrastructure, escalate privileges, and cause significant damage. MFA mitigates this risk by introducing additional verification steps that make unauthorized access more difficult.

One of the most effective MFA implementations for PAM is the use of time-based one-time passwords (TOTP). This method generates a temporary numeric code that changes every few seconds, ensuring that even if an attacker intercepts a code, it quickly becomes invalid. TOTP can be delivered through hardware tokens, mobile authentication apps, or SMS messages, though SMS-based MFA is considered less secure due to the risk of SIM swapping and man-in-the-middle attacks.

Biometric authentication is another powerful MFA mechanism for privileged accounts. Fingerprint scanning, facial recognition, and iris scanning provide high levels of security by relying on unique biological characteristics. Unlike passwords, biometrics cannot be easily shared or stolen. However, organizations must carefully manage biometric data to prevent privacy concerns and ensure compliance with data protection regulations.

Adaptive authentication, also known as risk-based authentication, further enhances PAM security by evaluating contextual factors before granting access. This approach considers elements such as the user's location, device type, login time, and behavior patterns. If a privileged user attempts to log in from an unfamiliar location or an untrusted device, the system may prompt for additional authentication or deny access altogether. Adaptive authentication adds a dynamic layer of security that adjusts based on real-time risk assessments.

Privileged session authentication should also incorporate MFA to prevent unauthorized access during active sessions. If a session remains idle for an extended period, the system can prompt the user to re-authenticate using MFA before resuming activities. This prevents attackers from exploiting unattended sessions to execute privileged actions without proper verification.

Integrating MFA with a PAM solution enhances centralized access control and simplifies security management. Modern PAM platforms support seamless MFA integration with identity providers, single sign-on (SSO) solutions, and security information and event management (SIEM) systems. This integration allows organizations to enforce MFA policies consistently across all privileged accounts and monitor authentication events for potential threats.

Despite its security benefits, MFA implementation must balance security with usability. Overly complex authentication processes can frustrate users and lead to security workarounds, such as writing down MFA codes or using unauthorized devices for authentication. Organizations should carefully design MFA policies to ensure security without disrupting productivity. This can be achieved through intelligent MFA strategies, such as requiring MFA only for high-risk transactions, using biometric authentication for ease of use, and implementing passwordless authentication methods.

Regulatory frameworks and industry standards mandate MFA as a critical security control for privileged accounts. Compliance requirements such as GDPR, PCI DSS, HIPAA, and NIST cybersecurity guidelines emphasize the importance of strong authentication for protecting sensitive data. Organizations that fail to implement MFA for privileged access may face regulatory penalties, data breaches, and reputational damage.

MFA is an essential layer of security in PAM, significantly reducing the likelihood of unauthorized access to privileged accounts. By combining multiple authentication factors, integrating adaptive authentication, and aligning with regulatory standards, organizations can protect their most critical assets from cyber threats. As attackers continue to develop new techniques for bypassing traditional authentication, MFA remains a powerful defense mechanism in securing privileged access.

Password Management and Vaulting

Password management and vaulting are critical components of Privileged Access Management (PAM), ensuring that privileged credentials are securely stored, managed, and protected from unauthorized access. Privileged accounts, which have elevated permissions to access sensitive systems and data, are high-value targets for cybercriminals. Without proper password management controls, organizations risk credential theft, unauthorized access, and security breaches. Implementing strong password policies, enforcing automated password rotation, and utilizing secure vaulting solutions significantly reduce these risks and enhance overall security posture.

One of the biggest challenges in managing privileged account passwords is the reliance on static credentials. Many organizations still use shared, manually managed passwords for administrative accounts, creating a security risk. Static passwords are vulnerable to brute force attacks, credential stuffing, and phishing attempts. Additionally, employees may reuse passwords across multiple systems, increasing the risk of credential compromise. To address these challenges, organizations must enforce strict password policies that include complexity requirements, expiration intervals, and unique password generation.

A key feature of effective password management is automated password rotation. Instead of relying on human intervention, PAM solutions can automatically rotate passwords at predefined intervals, ensuring that privileged credentials remain secure. Automated rotation eliminates the risks associated with long-lived passwords, making it harder for attackers to exploit compromised credentials. Additionally, password rotation can be enforced after each use, preventing credentials from being reused or shared.

Password vaulting is another essential security measure that helps organizations manage privileged credentials securely. A password vault is a centralized, encrypted repository that stores privileged account passwords, ensuring they are protected from unauthorized access. Vaulting solutions not only store passwords securely but also control access to them, ensuring that only authorized users can retrieve credentials when necessary. This approach prevents users from knowing or reusing privileged passwords, reducing the risk of credential exposure.

Modern password vaults integrate with authentication mechanisms such as multi-factor authentication (MFA) to add an extra layer of security. Before accessing privileged credentials, users must verify their identity through multiple authentication factors, such as biometrics, one-time passcodes, or hardware security tokens. This additional security measure ensures that even if a password is compromised, unauthorized users cannot gain access without proper verification.

Another important aspect of password vaulting is session management. PAM solutions can integrate password vaults with privileged session management (PSM) tools to establish secure, monitored sessions without exposing passwords to end users. Instead of users manually entering credentials, the PAM solution injects passwords into privileged sessions, ensuring that credentials remain protected. This approach minimizes the risk of password leaks and unauthorized credential sharing.

Auditing and logging are critical components of password management and vaulting. Organizations must maintain detailed logs of all password access attempts, including who accessed a password, when it was used, and for what purpose. This level of visibility enables security teams to detect unauthorized access attempts, investigate suspicious activities, and enforce compliance with regulatory requirements. Logs and audit trails also support forensic investigations in the event of a security incident.

Regulatory compliance frameworks such as PCI DSS, GDPR, and NIST emphasize the importance of password security for protecting sensitive data. These regulations require organizations to implement strong password policies, enforce periodic password changes, and maintain access control logs. By leveraging password vaulting and automated password management, organizations can ensure compliance with these standards while reducing the risk of data breaches.

Despite the security benefits of password management and vaulting, organizations must also focus on user education and awareness. Employees should be trained on best practices for managing passwords, recognizing phishing attempts, and following secure authentication procedures. While technology plays a crucial role in securing privileged credentials, human behavior remains a critical factor in preventing security breaches.

Password management and vaulting are essential for securing privileged access and reducing the risk of credential-based attacks. By implementing automated password rotation, enforcing strict password policies, integrating authentication mechanisms, and maintaining audit trails, organizations can protect their most critical assets from unauthorized access. As cyber threats continue to evolve, effective password management remains a fundamental defense against credential compromise and privilege abuse.

Rotating and Updating Privileged Credentials

Rotating and updating privileged credentials is a fundamental security practice that ensures sensitive accounts remain protected against unauthorized access, credential theft, and cyberattacks. Privileged accounts, which provide elevated access to critical systems, databases, and administrative functions, are often the primary targets of attackers. If these credentials are not frequently changed, they can be exploited for extended periods, allowing malicious actors to move laterally within an organization's infrastructure. Implementing a structured approach to credential rotation and updates significantly reduces the risk of unauthorized access while maintaining operational security.

One of the main reasons for regularly rotating privileged credentials is to limit the window of opportunity for attackers who may have gained access to them. When passwords or cryptographic keys remain unchanged for long durations, they become vulnerable to brute-force attacks, credential stuffing, and insider threats. By enforcing frequent updates, organizations can ensure that even if a credential is compromised, its usefulness is short-lived, preventing attackers from maintaining persistent access.

Automated credential rotation is a key component of an effective Privileged Access Management (PAM) strategy. Manual password changes are prone to human error, inconsistency, and delays, which can lead to gaps in security. Automated PAM solutions can enforce scheduled password rotations across all privileged accounts, ensuring that credentials are updated systematically and according to security policies. These systems also generate strong, complex passwords that meet security best practices, eliminating weak or reused credentials that could be easily guessed or cracked.

Service accounts and application credentials present unique challenges when it comes to rotation. These accounts are often embedded within scripts, configuration files, and applications, making password changes complex and prone to operational disruptions. Organizations must implement credential management solutions that seamlessly update stored credentials across all integrated systems to prevent authentication failures. Secure API-based credential storage, combined with automated rotation policies, ensures that application and service account credentials remain up to date without causing service interruptions.

Just-In-Time (JIT) access further enhances security by eliminating the need for persistent privileged credentials. Instead of maintaining static passwords that require rotation, JIT access provisions temporary credentials that expire after use. This approach minimizes the risk of long-term credential exposure and significantly reduces the attack surface. When JIT access is combined with multi-factor authentication (MFA), it strengthens security by ensuring that privileged access is granted only to authorized users when needed.

Cryptographic keys, SSH keys, and API tokens also require regular rotation to prevent unauthorized access. Many organizations rely on SSH keys for secure remote access, but failing to rotate these keys can result in untraceable and persistent access by former employees, contractors, or attackers who have obtained a copy. Implementing an automated key management system ensures that keys are periodically regenerated and replaced while enforcing strict access controls on key distribution and usage.

Compliance regulations and security frameworks emphasize the importance of credential rotation as part of a robust cybersecurity strategy. Standards such as NIST, PCI DSS, and ISO 27001 mandate periodic password changes for privileged accounts, ensuring that credentials do not remain static for extended periods. Organizations that fail to comply with these regulations risk security vulnerabilities, financial penalties, and reputational damage. Regular auditing and reporting on credential rotation activities help organizations demonstrate compliance and maintain accountability for privileged access security.

Human error remains one of the biggest risks in credential management. Users may inadvertently store privileged credentials in insecure locations, such as text files, emails, or shared documents.

Implementing a secure vaulting system prevents unauthorized access to stored credentials and enforces encryption for all privileged passwords. Role-based access controls (RBAC) further restrict who can retrieve, update, or manage credentials, ensuring that only authorized personnel have access to sensitive information.

Monitoring and logging credential rotation activities are essential for detecting anomalies and preventing potential security breaches. PAM solutions provide detailed logs of all credential updates, including timestamps, request origins, and access attempts. If an unauthorized change or suspicious activity is detected, security teams can take immediate action to revoke compromised credentials and investigate the source of the incident.

Organizations must continuously evaluate their credential rotation policies and update them as threats evolve. As cyberattacks become more sophisticated, relying solely on periodic password changes may not be sufficient. Advanced techniques such as passwordless authentication, biometric verification, and behavioral analytics can complement credential rotation strategies to enhance security further. By adopting a proactive approach to privileged credential management, organizations can safeguard their most critical assets and reduce the risk of unauthorized access.

Secure Session Management

Secure session management is a critical component of Privileged Access Management (PAM) that ensures privileged accounts are protected during active use. While strong authentication and access controls prevent unauthorized access, session management safeguards ongoing privileged activities, reducing the risk of credential theft, unauthorized actions, and session hijacking. Without proper session security, attackers can exploit vulnerabilities in active sessions to escalate privileges, execute malicious commands, or exfiltrate sensitive data. Implementing secure session management mechanisms helps organizations monitor, control, and protect privileged access in real time.

One of the most significant threats to privileged sessions is session hijacking. Attackers use techniques such as man-in-the-middle (MITM) attacks, session fixation, and stolen authentication tokens to gain control of an active session. Once inside, they can operate as a legitimate privileged user, making their actions difficult to detect. To mitigate these risks, organizations must implement encrypted session protocols, such as Secure Shell (SSH) and Transport Layer Security (TLS), which prevent unauthorized interception and tampering with privileged sessions.

Privileged session monitoring is an essential security measure that enables real-time visibility into privileged user activities. PAM solutions provide live session tracking, allowing security teams to observe user behavior, detect anomalies, and intervene if suspicious actions are detected. By implementing session recording, organizations create an audit trail that can be reviewed for compliance, forensic investigations, and security analysis. This approach ensures that every command executed within a privileged session is documented and auditable.

Session timeouts and automatic logouts help prevent unauthorized access to idle sessions. If a privileged session remains inactive for a predefined period, it should automatically terminate to minimize the risk of unauthorized use. This measure prevents attackers from exploiting unattended sessions, particularly in environments where users leave their workstations without logging out. Implementing session re-authentication further enhances security by requiring users to verify their identity before resuming an inactive session.

Just-In-Time (JIT) access is another effective method for secure session management. Instead of maintaining always-on privileged sessions, JIT access provisions temporary sessions that automatically expire after a specific duration. This approach minimizes the attack surface by ensuring that privileged access is granted only when necessary and for a limited period. By integrating JIT access with multi-factor authentication (MFA), organizations can further strengthen session security.

Session isolation is a technique that prevents privileged users from directly accessing critical systems without passing through a secure gateway. A PAM solution can act as a session broker, establishing a secure connection between the user and the target system without exposing credentials. This method ensures that privileged users do not have direct access to sensitive systems, reducing the risk of lateral movement in the event of a compromised session.

Implementing strong endpoint security measures is essential for maintaining session integrity. Privileged users accessing systems from unsecured or compromised devices pose a significant risk to session security. Organizations should enforce endpoint security policies that require privileged users to connect only from trusted devices that comply with security standards. This includes using corporate-managed devices, implementing endpoint detection and response (EDR) solutions, and restricting access from public or untrusted networks.

Privileged session shadowing is a proactive security measure that allows security administrators to observe user activities in real time. If an administrator detects unusual behavior, they can take immediate action, such as terminating the session or revoking access. Shadowing is particularly useful for high-risk sessions, such as those involving third-party vendors or remote access to critical infrastructure.

Auditing and logging privileged sessions provide valuable insights into user behavior, access patterns, and potential security threats. Organizations must maintain detailed logs of all privileged sessions, including user activity, session duration, and executed commands. Integrating session logs with Security Information and Event Management (SIEM) solutions enables real-time threat detection, alerting security teams to anomalies that may indicate unauthorized access or privilege abuse.

Organizations must also consider compliance requirements when implementing secure session management. Regulatory frameworks such as GDPR, HIPAA, and PCI DSS mandate strict controls over privileged access, requiring organizations to monitor, record, and audit privileged sessions. Failure to comply with these regulations can result in financial penalties, legal consequences, and reputational damage.

PAM solutions help organizations meet compliance requirements by enforcing secure session policies, generating audit trails, and providing detailed reports for regulatory audits.

Secure session management is an ongoing process that requires continuous monitoring, policy enforcement, and adaptation to emerging threats. By implementing encryption, session monitoring, automatic timeouts, JIT access, and strong endpoint security, organizations can protect privileged sessions from unauthorized access and exploitation. Combining these measures with comprehensive auditing and compliance practices ensures that privileged access remains secure, controlled, and aligned with industry best practices.

Session Monitoring and Recording

Session monitoring and recording play a crucial role in Privileged Access Management (PAM), providing organizations with visibility into privileged user activities and ensuring accountability for administrative actions. Privileged accounts grant users elevated access to critical systems, databases, and sensitive information. Without proper monitoring, these accounts can be misused, either intentionally by malicious insiders or unintentionally due to human error. Implementing a robust session monitoring and recording strategy helps detect unauthorized access, prevent security breaches, and support regulatory compliance.

Privileged session monitoring involves real-time tracking of user activities during an active session. This includes logging every action performed within a privileged account, such as executing commands, modifying configurations, and accessing sensitive data. By continuously monitoring privileged sessions, organizations can quickly detect and respond to suspicious behavior before it escalates into a security incident. Monitoring privileged access in real time also helps enforce security policies by ensuring that users adhere to established protocols when handling critical resources.

Session recording provides an additional layer of security by capturing a visual or textual representation of all privileged activities. Recorded sessions allow security teams to review actions taken within an administrative session, making it easier to investigate security incidents, detect policy violations, and provide evidence in forensic investigations. Many PAM solutions offer keystroke logging, video recording, and command tracking to ensure that every action performed by a privileged user is documented.

One of the key benefits of session monitoring and recording is the ability to deter insider threats. When users are aware that their activities are being monitored, they are less likely to engage in unauthorized behavior. This creates a culture of accountability, ensuring that privileged users follow security best practices and comply with access control policies. Additionally, if a security breach occurs, recorded sessions provide valuable evidence that can help security teams trace the source of the incident and mitigate its impact.

Session monitoring also helps organizations detect anomalous behavior that may indicate a compromised privileged account. For example, if an administrator logs in from an unusual location, performs actions outside of normal working hours, or executes unauthorized commands, security teams can receive real-time alerts and take immediate action. Advanced PAM solutions leverage artificial intelligence (AI) and machine learning to analyze session behavior, identifying patterns that deviate from normal user activity and flagging potential threats.

Regulatory compliance frameworks such as GDPR, PCI DSS, HIPAA, and NIST require organizations to implement session monitoring and auditing controls to protect sensitive data. These regulations mandate that privileged activities be logged and reviewed to prevent unauthorized access and ensure accountability. By maintaining detailed session recordings, organizations can demonstrate compliance with industry standards, avoid financial penalties, and strengthen their overall security posture.

Effective session recording requires secure storage and access controls to prevent unauthorized tampering or deletion. Recorded sessions should be encrypted and stored in a centralized, tamper-proof archive, ensuring that they remain intact for audit and forensic purposes. Access to recorded sessions must be restricted to authorized personnel, with strict role-based access control (RBAC) policies in place to prevent misuse.

Balancing security and privacy is another important consideration when implementing session monitoring. While organizations need visibility into privileged activities, they must also comply with privacy regulations that protect user data. Session monitoring policies should clearly define what activities are recorded, who has access to session logs, and how long recordings are retained. Transparency in monitoring practices helps build trust among employees while maintaining a strong security framework.

Integrating session monitoring with Security Information and Event Management (SIEM) systems enhances threat detection and incident response. SIEM solutions aggregate logs from various sources, allowing security teams to correlate privileged session activities with other security events. This integration provides a comprehensive view of potential threats, enabling faster detection and mitigation of security incidents.

Automating session monitoring and recording through PAM solutions reduces the burden on security teams while ensuring consistent enforcement of security policies. Automated alerts and behavioral analytics enable organizations to proactively detect and respond to privileged account misuse, minimizing the risk of data breaches.

Session monitoring and recording are essential components of a robust PAM strategy. By continuously tracking privileged activities, enforcing accountability, and integrating with security solutions, organizations can effectively protect their critical assets from insider threats, unauthorized access, and compliance violations. A well-implemented monitoring system strengthens security defenses, reduces operational risks, and ensures that privileged access remains under strict control.

Auditing and Reporting on Privileged Activities

Auditing and reporting on privileged activities are essential components of Privileged Access Management (PAM), ensuring that organizations maintain visibility, accountability, and compliance in managing privileged accounts. Privileged users, such as system administrators and IT personnel, have access to critical systems and sensitive data, making their actions a high-risk area for security breaches, insider threats, and regulatory violations. A comprehensive auditing and reporting strategy enables organizations to detect unauthorized activities, respond to security incidents, and meet compliance requirements.

The primary objective of privileged activity auditing is to provide a detailed record of all actions performed by privileged users. This includes login attempts, configuration changes, data access, and administrative operations. Without proper auditing mechanisms, organizations lack insight into how privileged accounts are being used, leaving them vulnerable to security threats. A well-implemented audit framework ensures that every privileged action is logged, timestamped, and attributed to a specific user, reducing the risk of anonymous or untraceable activities.

Privileged access auditing also plays a crucial role in detecting anomalies and potential security breaches. By continuously monitoring privileged activities, organizations can identify suspicious patterns, such as repeated failed login attempts, access from unusual locations, or unauthorized privilege escalations. Modern PAM solutions incorporate artificial intelligence (AI) and machine learning to analyze audit logs and detect deviations from normal user behavior. When an anomaly is detected, automated alerts can be triggered to notify security teams, enabling rapid incident response and mitigation.

Regulatory compliance is another key driver for auditing and reporting on privileged activities. Various industry standards and government regulations, such as GDPR, HIPAA, PCI DSS, SOX, and NIST, require organizations to maintain audit trails for privileged access. These regulations mandate that organizations log, monitor, and report on privileged activities to ensure accountability and data protection. Failure to comply with these requirements can result in financial penalties, legal consequences, and reputational damage. An effective auditing framework provides the necessary documentation to demonstrate compliance during audits and regulatory inspections.

Generating audit reports is a critical function in privileged access governance. Reports provide summarized insights into privileged activity trends, access violations, and security events. Organizations can customize reports to focus on specific areas, such as login activity, privilege escalations, or unauthorized access attempts. Security teams, compliance officers, and executive leadership rely on these reports to assess security posture, enforce policy adherence, and make informed decisions about access controls.

Centralized logging is a best practice for auditing privileged activities. Instead of storing audit logs across multiple systems, a centralized PAM solution collects and aggregates all privileged activity logs in a secure repository. This centralized approach simplifies log analysis, enhances visibility, and ensures that logs cannot be tampered with or deleted by malicious insiders. Integration with Security Information and Event Management (SIEM) systems further enhances audit capabilities, allowing organizations to correlate privileged access events with broader security incidents.

Access review and certification processes are closely linked to privileged activity auditing. Regular access reviews help organizations validate whether users still require their existing privileges. By analyzing audit logs, security teams can identify inactive accounts, unnecessary privilege escalations, or violations of access policies. Automated workflows can facilitate periodic access certifications, ensuring that privileged access remains aligned with business needs and security policies.

Organizations must also implement audit retention policies to determine how long privileged activity logs should be stored. Regulatory frameworks often specify retention requirements, ranging from several months to multiple years. Secure storage and encryption of audit logs are critical to preventing unauthorized access or tampering. Organizations should also establish clear policies on who has access to audit logs and reporting tools, ensuring that sensitive information remains protected.

Continuous improvement in privileged activity auditing is necessary to adapt to evolving security threats. Regular audits of privileged access policies, log analysis, and incident investigations provide insights into potential vulnerabilities and areas for enhancement. Organizations should update their auditing and reporting mechanisms based on emerging cybersecurity trends, regulatory changes, and lessons learned from past security incidents.

Auditing and reporting on privileged activities provide organizations with the visibility and control needed to secure privileged access effectively. By implementing robust logging, monitoring, anomaly detection, and compliance reporting, organizations can mitigate security risks, prevent unauthorized access, and maintain trust in their privileged access management framework.

Compliance and Regulatory Considerations

Compliance and regulatory considerations are critical components of Privileged Access Management (PAM), ensuring that organizations meet legal, industry, and security requirements while protecting sensitive data. Regulatory frameworks impose strict access control, monitoring, and auditing requirements to prevent unauthorized access, data breaches, and cyber threats. Organizations that fail to comply with these regulations risk financial penalties, legal consequences, and reputational damage. Implementing a robust PAM strategy aligned with regulatory mandates helps organizations maintain security, accountability, and operational integrity.

Many global and industry-specific regulations emphasize the need for strong privileged access controls. The General Data Protection Regulation (GDPR), for instance, requires organizations handling EU citizens' personal data to implement stringent security measures, including access restrictions and audit logging. Under GDPR, organizations must demonstrate that only authorized personnel can access sensitive data and that privileged activities are logged for forensic and compliance purposes. Failure to comply with GDPR can result in heavy fines, making PAM a critical tool for organizations that store and process personal data.

Similarly, the Payment Card Industry Data Security Standard (PCI DSS) mandates strict privileged access controls to protect payment card information. PCI DSS requires organizations to enforce role-based access control (RBAC), implement multi-factor authentication (MFA) for privileged accounts, and monitor all administrative activities. By integrating PAM solutions, organizations can meet PCI DSS requirements by ensuring that only authorized users access payment card environments while maintaining detailed logs of privileged activities.

The Health Insurance Portability and Accountability Act (HIPAA) sets security and privacy requirements for healthcare organizations handling protected health information (PHI). HIPAA mandates that healthcare providers, insurers, and business associates implement access controls, session monitoring, and audit logs to prevent unauthorized access to patient records. PAM solutions help healthcare organizations enforce least privilege principles, track privileged activities, and respond to potential security incidents, ensuring compliance with HIPAA regulations.

For financial institutions, the Sarbanes-Oxley Act (SOX) establishes strict controls to prevent fraud and ensure the integrity of financial reporting. SOX compliance requires organizations to maintain detailed access logs, implement privileged account monitoring, and conduct regular audits of financial systems. PAM plays a crucial role in SOX compliance by providing visibility into privileged access, enforcing access restrictions, and generating audit-ready reports that demonstrate compliance with financial regulations.

The National Institute of Standards and Technology (NIST) provides cybersecurity frameworks that outline best practices for privileged access security. NIST Special Publication 800-53, for example, includes specific controls for managing privileged accounts, enforcing strong authentication, and maintaining audit trails. Organizations that adopt

NIST guidelines strengthen their cybersecurity posture while aligning with government and industry security standards.

The Federal Risk and Authorization Management Program (FedRAMP) applies to cloud service providers working with U.S. federal agencies. FedRAMP mandates strict privileged access controls, requiring cloud providers to implement PAM solutions that secure administrative accounts, enforce session monitoring, and prevent unauthorized access to government data. Compliance with FedRAMP ensures that cloud environments meet high security standards while protecting sensitive government information.

Privileged access compliance also extends to emerging cybersecurity laws and industry regulations. The Cybersecurity Maturity Model Certification (CMMC), introduced by the U.S. Department of Defense, requires defense contractors to implement privileged access controls as part of their cybersecurity programs. Similarly, the ISO/IEC 27001 standard outlines best practices for securing information assets, including strict privileged access controls, continuous monitoring, and risk management processes.

Auditability and reporting are key aspects of compliance in PAM. Regulations require organizations to maintain detailed records of privileged access activities, including who accessed sensitive systems, when, and what actions were performed. PAM solutions generate automated audit logs and reports, providing organizations with real-time insights into privileged activities. These records help demonstrate compliance with regulatory requirements while enabling security teams to detect and respond to potential threats.

Many compliance frameworks require organizations to conduct regular access reviews to verify that privileged access remains justified and necessary. Periodic access certification ensures that privileges are granted based on business needs and revoked when no longer required. PAM solutions streamline this process by providing automated workflows for reviewing, approving, and revoking privileged access.

Organizations must also address third-party access compliance. Many regulations require strict controls for vendors, contractors, and external partners who require privileged access to critical systems.

PAM solutions enforce time-restricted, just-in-time (JIT) access for third parties, ensuring that external users only receive access when necessary and for a limited duration. Continuous monitoring of third-party privileged sessions further reduces security risks and supports compliance with regulatory mandates.

Data protection regulations continue to evolve, requiring organizations to adapt their privileged access security practices accordingly. Compliance is not just about avoiding penalties but also about building trust with customers, partners, and stakeholders. By implementing a PAM strategy that aligns with regulatory requirements, organizations enhance security, maintain operational resilience, and ensure that privileged access remains secure, auditable, and compliant with industry standards.

Integrating PAM into Existing IT Environments

Integrating Privileged Access Management (PAM) into an existing IT environment is a complex but necessary process for enhancing security, protecting sensitive data, and reducing the risk of unauthorized access. Many organizations operate in hybrid environments that include on-premises infrastructure, cloud services, legacy systems, and third-party applications, all of which require privileged access controls. Implementing PAM effectively in these environments ensures that privileged accounts are properly managed, monitored, and secured without disrupting business operations.

The first challenge organizations face when integrating PAM is identifying all privileged accounts and access points within their existing infrastructure. Many IT environments contain a mix of administrative accounts, service accounts, application credentials, and shared privileged accounts that have accumulated over time. Conducting a thorough discovery process helps organizations catalog these accounts, assess their access levels, and determine which accounts pose the highest security risks. Without full visibility, privileged access can remain unmanaged, leading to potential security vulnerabilities.

Once privileged accounts are identified, organizations must define and enforce policies that align with security best practices. The principle of least privilege (PoLP) is a fundamental concept in PAM, ensuring that users and systems have only the minimum level of access necessary to perform their tasks. Implementing role-based access control (RBAC) and just-in-time (JIT) privilege escalation further enhances security by restricting access based on job roles and limiting the duration of privileged access. These policies should be applied consistently across all systems, including on-premises servers, cloud platforms, and remote access environments.

One of the critical steps in PAM integration is implementing a centralized authentication mechanism that supports multi-factor authentication (MFA) for privileged users. Traditional authentication methods, such as static passwords, are insufficient for securing privileged accounts. PAM solutions provide secure vaulting for privileged credentials, ensuring that passwords are stored, rotated, and accessed securely. Automated password management eliminates the need for users to manually manage credentials, reducing the risk of password leaks and credential-based attacks.

Another key aspect of PAM integration is privileged session management. Organizations must ensure that all privileged activities are monitored, recorded, and auditable. Session monitoring tools track user actions in real-time, allowing security teams to detect anomalies and respond to potential threats. Privileged session recording provides a detailed audit trail for compliance purposes and forensic investigations. By integrating PAM with security information and event management (SIEM) systems, organizations can correlate privileged activity logs with broader security events, improving threat detection and incident response.

Legacy systems pose unique challenges when integrating PAM, as many older applications and infrastructure components were not designed with modern security controls in mind. Some legacy systems may rely on hardcoded credentials, lack support for MFA, or have limited logging capabilities. Organizations must develop strategies to extend PAM security controls to these systems, such as using API-based credential management, implementing proxy-based access controls, or deploying secure gateways to mediate privileged access.

Cloud environments introduce additional complexities when integrating PAM, as cloud service providers often use different identity and access management (IAM) frameworks. PAM solutions must be adapted to support cloud-based workloads, including infrastructure-as-a-service (IaaS), platform-as-a-service (PaaS), and software-as-a-service (SaaS) environments. Secure integration with cloud-native authentication methods, such as AWS IAM roles or Azure Active Directory, ensures that privileged access is managed consistently across both on-premises and cloud resources.

Automating PAM policies and workflows helps organizations maintain security while reducing administrative overhead. PAM solutions can integrate with IT service management (ITSM) platforms to streamline access approval processes, automate privilege escalations, and enforce policy compliance. Automated workflows ensure that privileged access requests are reviewed, approved, and logged systematically, minimizing the risk of unauthorized privilege assignments.

User training and awareness are essential when integrating PAM into an existing IT environment. Many security breaches result from human errors, such as credential sharing, weak password practices, or misconfigurations. Educating employees, administrators, and third-party vendors on PAM policies, security best practices, and compliance requirements strengthens the organization's overall security posture. Additionally, ongoing security awareness programs help reinforce the importance of privileged access security and encourage adherence to established protocols.

Regular audits and assessments ensure that PAM integration remains effective over time. Organizations should conduct periodic privileged access reviews to verify that users and systems have the correct level of access. Access logs and audit trails should be analyzed to identify anomalies, detect privilege creep, and refine security policies. By continuously evaluating PAM effectiveness, organizations can adapt to evolving threats and maintain compliance with industry regulations and security standards.

Integrating PAM into an existing IT environment requires a comprehensive strategy that includes privileged account discovery, policy enforcement, authentication enhancements, session monitoring, legacy system support, cloud integration, automation, user training, and ongoing auditing. By systematically implementing these measures, organizations can effectively secure privileged access, reduce attack surfaces, and strengthen overall cybersecurity resilience.

Managing Privileged Access in the Cloud

The widespread adoption of cloud computing has transformed how organizations manage their IT infrastructure, data, and applications. While the cloud offers scalability, flexibility, and cost-efficiency, it also introduces new security challenges, particularly in managing privileged access. Unlike traditional on-premises environments, where organizations have direct control over physical servers and networks, cloud environments rely on shared responsibility models, requiring organizations to implement strict access controls to protect sensitive resources. Privileged Access Management (PAM) in the cloud is essential to prevent unauthorized access, reduce the risk of data breaches, and ensure compliance with industry regulations.

One of the primary challenges in managing privileged access in the cloud is the dynamic nature of cloud workloads. Cloud environments often involve a mix of Infrastructure-as-a-Service (IaaS), Platform-as-a-Service (PaaS), and Software-as-a-Service (SaaS) solutions, each with its own set of access control mechanisms. Administrators must manage privileged access across multiple platforms, including public cloud providers such as Amazon Web Services (AWS), Microsoft Azure, and Google Cloud Platform (GCP). Each cloud service operates differently, requiring organizations to adopt a unified PAM strategy that enforces consistent security policies across all cloud environments.

Another significant risk in cloud environments is the overuse of long-lived privileged credentials. Many organizations rely on static access keys, API tokens, and service accounts to facilitate automated processes and integrations. If these credentials are not regularly rotated or secured, they become a high-value target for cyber attackers. Implementing Just-In-Time (JIT) access reduces this risk by provisioning temporary credentials that expire after use, ensuring that privileged accounts are only active when needed. This minimizes the attack surface and prevents unauthorized access in case credentials are compromised.

Multi-Factor Authentication (MFA) is a critical security measure for managing privileged access in the cloud. MFA adds an extra layer of security by requiring users to verify their identity using multiple factors, such as passwords, biometric authentication, or hardware tokens. Cloud service providers offer built-in MFA solutions, but organizations should enforce MFA policies consistently across all privileged accounts, including administrative accounts, cloud consoles, and remote access points.

Role-Based Access Control (RBAC) and Attribute-Based Access Control (ABAC) are essential frameworks for managing privileged access in the cloud. RBAC assigns permissions based on predefined roles, ensuring that users only have the access necessary for their job functions. ABAC extends this model by incorporating additional attributes, such as device type, location, and time of access, to enforce more granular access controls. Implementing RBAC and ABAC helps organizations reduce privilege creep and enforce the principle of least privilege (PoLP).

Privileged session monitoring is another key aspect of cloud PAM. Cloud environments lack the traditional network perimeters that protect on-premises systems, making it crucial to monitor privileged user activity in real time. Session monitoring solutions record user actions within cloud management consoles, virtual machines, and privileged access gateways, providing visibility into administrative activities. If suspicious behavior is detected, automated alerts can trigger incident response mechanisms to prevent potential security breaches.

Organizations must also consider third-party access when managing privileged access in the cloud. Many enterprises rely on cloud service providers, consultants, and managed service providers (MSPs) to support their cloud operations. Granting unrestricted access to third parties increases security risks, making it essential to enforce strict access policies. Implementing time-restricted access, session monitoring, and approval workflows ensures that third-party users only have the permissions required for their tasks and that their activities are logged for security audits.

Compliance and regulatory considerations are another driving force behind cloud PAM adoption. Regulations such as GDPR, HIPAA, PCI DSS, and ISO 27001 require organizations to implement strong access controls, maintain audit logs, and protect sensitive data in the cloud. PAM solutions help organizations meet these compliance requirements by enforcing least privilege access, providing real-time monitoring, and generating detailed audit reports. Ensuring that privileged access policies align with industry standards reduces the risk of regulatory penalties and enhances security governance.

Automating privileged access management is crucial for securing cloud environments. Cloud-native PAM solutions integrate with identity and access management (IAM) services to automate access provisioning, credential rotation, and compliance reporting. Automation reduces the administrative burden on IT teams, improves security consistency, and minimizes human errors that could lead to security vulnerabilities. By leveraging artificial intelligence and machine learning, organizations can enhance threat detection, identifying abnormal access patterns and responding to potential security incidents in real time.

As organizations continue to migrate workloads to the cloud, securing privileged access remains a top priority. By implementing JIT access, MFA, RBAC, privileged session monitoring, and automation, organizations can protect cloud environments from unauthorized access and insider threats. A strong cloud PAM strategy ensures that privileged accounts are managed effectively, reducing security risks while maintaining compliance and operational efficiency.

PAM for DevOps and CI/CD Pipelines

Privileged Access Management (PAM) plays a crucial role in securing DevOps environments and Continuous Integration/Continuous Deployment (CI/CD) pipelines. DevOps practices emphasize automation, rapid development cycles, and frequent deployments, making it essential to manage privileged access effectively. Without robust PAM controls, organizations risk unauthorized access to critical infrastructure, credential exposure, and security breaches that can compromise the entire software development lifecycle.

One of the biggest security challenges in DevOps environments is the widespread use of automated processes that require elevated privileges. Build servers, deployment tools, and configuration management systems often rely on privileged credentials to interact with cloud environments, code repositories, and production servers. If these credentials are hardcoded into scripts or stored in unsecured locations, they become prime targets for attackers. Implementing PAM solutions ensures that privileged credentials are securely stored, rotated, and accessed only when necessary.

A key aspect of securing DevOps pipelines is integrating PAM with secret management tools. Developers and automated systems frequently need access to API keys, SSH keys, and database credentials. Instead of embedding secrets in source code or environment variables, organizations should use dedicated secret management solutions that enforce access control and auditing. PAM systems can integrate with these tools to provide centralized management of privileged credentials, ensuring that only authorized processes can retrieve them.

Just-in-Time (JIT) access is an effective strategy for reducing the exposure of privileged accounts in DevOps workflows. Instead of granting persistent administrative privileges to users or systems, JIT access provisions temporary access on demand, reducing the attack surface. This approach is particularly useful in CI/CD pipelines, where access to production environments should be granted only when needed and revoked immediately after use. Automating JIT access through PAM solutions ensures that privilege escalation is strictly controlled and monitored.

Privileged session monitoring is another critical component of PAM for DevOps. Many DevOps engineers and system administrators require direct access to production systems for troubleshooting and deployment tasks. Without proper session monitoring, these activities can go untracked, increasing the risk of misconfigurations and insider threats. PAM solutions enable real-time monitoring and recording of privileged sessions, allowing security teams to review actions taken during deployments and respond to suspicious behavior.

Role-Based Access Control (RBAC) and Attribute-Based Access Control (ABAC) should be enforced across DevOps tools and CI/CD pipelines to minimize privilege sprawl. Instead of granting broad administrative access to all DevOps team members, organizations should define roles based on job responsibilities and enforce least privilege access. ABAC extends this approach by incorporating contextual factors such as user location, time of access, and device security posture to determine access rights dynamically.

CI/CD pipelines rely heavily on third-party integrations, including cloud services, container orchestration platforms, and code repositories. Each of these integrations requires secure authentication mechanisms to prevent unauthorized access. PAM solutions help organizations enforce strong authentication policies, such as multi-factor authentication (MFA) and machine identity management, ensuring that only trusted entities can interact with CI/CD workflows.

Another important consideration is securing infrastructure as code (IaC) deployments. Tools like Terraform, Ansible, and Kubernetes require elevated privileges to provision and manage cloud resources. If not properly secured, these tools can be exploited to gain unauthorized access to sensitive environments. PAM solutions can integrate with IaC workflows to enforce access controls, audit changes, and prevent privilege abuse.

Auditing and compliance are essential aspects of PAM in DevOps environments. Regulatory frameworks such as GDPR, PCI DSS, and ISO 27001 require organizations to track and manage privileged access to critical systems. PAM solutions generate detailed audit logs that provide visibility into privileged activities within CI/CD pipelines, ensuring that security teams can detect anomalies and maintain compliance with industry regulations.

By integrating PAM into DevOps and CI/CD pipelines, organizations can mitigate security risks while maintaining the agility and efficiency of software development. Secure credential management, JIT access, session monitoring, RBAC enforcement, and compliance reporting all contribute to a robust security framework that protects privileged access in highly automated environments. As DevOps practices continue to evolve, implementing PAM controls will remain a critical priority for securing modern development workflows.

Privileged Access for Third-Party Vendors

Third-party vendors play a critical role in modern business operations, providing services such as IT support, cloud infrastructure management, software development, and system maintenance. While these vendors help organizations operate efficiently, they also introduce significant security risks, particularly when granted privileged access to sensitive systems. Without proper controls, third-party access can become a major attack vector, leading to data breaches, compliance violations, and financial losses. Implementing a robust Privileged Access Management (PAM) strategy for third-party vendors ensures that external users only receive the access necessary to perform their tasks while minimizing security risks.

One of the biggest challenges with third-party privileged access is the lack of direct oversight. Unlike internal employees, vendors operate outside the organization's security perimeter, often using their own devices and networks to access critical systems. This makes it difficult to enforce security policies consistently. Organizations must implement strict authentication mechanisms, such as multi-factor authentication (MFA), to verify vendor identities before granting access. Enforcing MFA across all third-party accounts reduces the likelihood of unauthorized access, even if a vendor's credentials are compromised.

Granting vendors excessive or permanent privileged access creates additional risks. Many organizations fall into the trap of providing persistent administrative credentials to third parties for convenience, leading to privilege creep. Just-In-Time (JIT) access is an effective solution to this problem. Instead of maintaining continuous privileged access, JIT access grants vendors temporary credentials only when needed and revokes them once the task is completed. This approach reduces the attack surface and prevents unauthorized access when vendor accounts are not actively in use.

Privileged session monitoring is another essential security measure when managing third-party vendor access. By recording and tracking all privileged activities performed by external users, organizations can ensure accountability and detect any suspicious actions. Session monitoring tools allow security teams to observe vendor activities in real time and generate alerts for unusual behavior, such as unauthorized file transfers, system modifications, or attempts to escalate privileges. Implementing session recording also provides valuable audit logs that can be reviewed for compliance and forensic investigations.

Establishing strict access approval workflows ensures that vendors do not gain unrestricted access to critical systems. Access requests should go through a formal approval process, involving IT administrators, security teams, and business stakeholders. Role-based access control (RBAC) and attribute-based access control (ABAC) models further refine permissions by limiting vendor access based on job function, time of access, and specific tasks. These controls help prevent third-party users from gaining unnecessary privileges that could be exploited by attackers.

Third-party vendor access must also be aligned with regulatory requirements. Compliance frameworks such as GDPR, HIPAA, PCI DSS, and ISO 27001 mandate strict controls over privileged access to protect sensitive data. Organizations must maintain audit logs of all vendor activities, enforce least privilege principles, and conduct regular access reviews to ensure compliance. Failure to implement these controls can result in regulatory penalties and reputational damage.

Automating third-party privileged access management helps organizations enforce security policies consistently. PAM solutions integrate with identity and access management (IAM) platforms to streamline vendor onboarding, enforce password vaulting, and automate access reviews. By reducing manual intervention, automation enhances security while improving operational efficiency.

Ongoing vendor risk assessments are necessary to maintain a secure privileged access framework. Organizations should evaluate vendor security policies, conduct penetration testing, and enforce contractual agreements that mandate compliance with security best practices. Regular audits and security reviews ensure that third-party access remains tightly controlled and aligned with the organization's risk management strategy.

By implementing strong authentication, just-in-time access, session monitoring, and automated security controls, organizations can effectively manage privileged access for third-party vendors. These measures protect sensitive data, reduce security risks, and ensure compliance with regulatory standards, allowing businesses to leverage external expertise without compromising security.

Addressing Insider Threats with PAM

Insider threats represent one of the most complex and challenging security risks for organizations. Unlike external attackers who must breach perimeter defenses, insiders already have access to critical systems, making them difficult to detect and mitigate. Privileged Access Management (PAM) plays a vital role in reducing the risk of insider threats by enforcing strict access controls, monitoring privileged activities, and ensuring accountability for users with elevated permissions. Whether caused by malicious intent, negligence, or human error, insider threats can result in data breaches, financial losses, and reputational damage. Implementing PAM helps organizations prevent, detect, and respond to insider threats effectively.

Insider threats typically fall into three categories: malicious insiders, negligent insiders, and compromised insiders. Malicious insiders deliberately misuse their access for personal gain, sabotage, or corporate espionage. Negligent insiders unintentionally expose sensitive data or misconfigure systems, leading to security vulnerabilities. Compromised insiders are legitimate users whose accounts have been hijacked by external attackers through phishing, malware, or credential theft. PAM mitigates these risks by limiting user privileges, monitoring access behavior, and providing real-time visibility into privileged activities.

One of the most effective ways to prevent insider threats is by enforcing the principle of least privilege (PoLP). Granting users only the minimum access required for their job functions reduces the likelihood of privilege abuse. PAM solutions implement role-based access control (RBAC) and attribute-based access control (ABAC) to ensure that employees, contractors, and third-party vendors do not have excessive privileges. Regular access reviews and privilege audits help organizations identify and remove unnecessary access, reducing the risk of insider exploitation.

Multi-factor authentication (MFA) is a crucial security measure in preventing unauthorized access by insiders. Even if an insider's credentials are compromised, requiring an additional authentication factor, such as a biometric scan or one-time passcode, prevents unauthorized use of privileged accounts. PAM solutions enforce MFA for all privileged users, ensuring that only verified individuals can access critical systems and sensitive data.

Privileged session monitoring is another essential component of insider threat mitigation. By recording and tracking privileged activities in real time, PAM provides security teams with insights into user behavior. Session monitoring enables organizations to detect unusual patterns, such as unauthorized data access, privilege escalation, or attempts to bypass security controls. If an insider attempts to perform suspicious activities, automated alerts can notify security teams, allowing them to respond before any damage is done.

Detecting insider threats also requires behavioral analytics and anomaly detection. PAM solutions leverage artificial intelligence (AI) and machine learning to analyze user behavior and identify deviations from normal activity. For example, if an employee suddenly accesses systems outside of their usual work hours or downloads large amounts of sensitive data, PAM can flag the activity for further investigation. By continuously analyzing privileged user behavior, organizations can proactively identify potential insider threats before they escalate.

Insider threats are not limited to employees; third-party vendors and contractors with privileged access can also pose risks. PAM enforces strict access controls for external users by implementing just-in-time (JIT) access, which grants temporary privileges only when needed. Once a task is completed, the access is automatically revoked, minimizing the risk of insider abuse. Continuous monitoring of third-party activities ensures that external users do not misuse their access or exceed their authorized permissions.

Data loss prevention (DLP) mechanisms integrated with PAM further enhance insider threat protection. Organizations can define policies that restrict sensitive data transfers, prevent unauthorized file downloads, and block access to high-risk systems. PAM solutions work alongside DLP tools to enforce security controls and mitigate data exfiltration attempts by insiders.

Incident response and forensic investigation capabilities are essential for addressing insider threats. PAM solutions maintain detailed audit logs and session recordings, providing security teams with evidence of privileged activities. If a security incident occurs, forensic analysis helps organizations determine the scope of the threat, identify the responsible insider, and implement corrective measures to prevent future occurrences.

Security awareness training is a crucial component of an effective insider threat mitigation strategy. Employees must be educated on security best practices, phishing risks, and the importance of following access control policies. PAM solutions provide security teams with insights into user behavior, allowing them to tailor training programs to address specific risks.

Organizations must adopt a proactive approach to managing insider threats by continuously assessing privileged access risks, refining security policies, and leveraging PAM solutions for real-time monitoring and threat detection. By enforcing least privilege access, implementing MFA, monitoring privileged sessions, and utilizing behavioral analytics, businesses can effectively mitigate insider threats and strengthen their overall security posture.

Incident Response and Breach Containment

Incident response and breach containment are critical components of a comprehensive cybersecurity strategy, particularly in the context of Privileged Access Management (PAM). When privileged accounts are compromised, attackers can gain deep access to critical systems, allowing them to manipulate configurations, exfiltrate sensitive data, or deploy ransomware. Without a well-defined incident response plan, organizations may struggle to contain breaches, leading to prolonged exposure, financial losses, and reputational damage. Establishing a structured approach to detecting, mitigating, and recovering from security incidents involving privileged access is essential for minimizing risks and restoring normal operations efficiently.

The first step in an effective incident response strategy is rapid detection. Security teams must continuously monitor privileged account activities for signs of unauthorized access, abnormal behavior, or privilege escalation. Indicators of compromise (IoCs) such as repeated failed login attempts, access from unusual locations, or changes to system configurations should trigger automated alerts. Integrating PAM solutions with Security Information and Event Management (SIEM) systems enhances real-time threat detection, allowing security analysts to quickly identify and investigate suspicious activities.

Once a security incident is detected, immediate containment measures must be initiated to prevent further damage. Privileged session isolation is a key tactic for limiting attacker movement within the network. By automatically terminating suspicious privileged sessions, organizations can prevent lateral movement and block attackers from escalating privileges. Just-In-Time (JIT) access controls further reduce exposure by ensuring that privileged credentials are only available when absolutely necessary, preventing attackers from exploiting long-standing administrative accounts.

Credential revocation and rotation are critical components of breach containment. If a privileged account is compromised, security teams must immediately disable affected credentials and issue new ones to prevent unauthorized reuse. Automated password rotation policies enforced by PAM solutions ensure that privileged credentials are updated regularly, reducing the likelihood of attackers maintaining persistent access. Additionally, organizations should enforce multi-factor authentication (MFA) across all privileged accounts to add an extra layer of security, making it more difficult for attackers to regain access.

Forensic investigation is essential for understanding the scope and impact of a security breach. Security teams must analyze privileged session logs, access histories, and system changes to determine how the attack was executed and what data may have been compromised. PAM solutions provide detailed audit trails that help investigators track attacker movements, identify vulnerabilities, and implement corrective actions. Conducting a thorough root cause analysis ensures that security gaps are addressed, preventing similar incidents in the future.

Effective communication and coordination are vital during incident response efforts. Organizations must establish predefined escalation paths and response teams to ensure a swift and organized approach to containment and remediation. Incident response teams should include cybersecurity specialists, IT administrators, legal advisors, and public relations personnel who can manage technical, legal, and reputational aspects of a breach. Clear communication with stakeholders, including customers and regulatory bodies, helps maintain transparency and trust while ensuring compliance with data breach notification requirements.

Recovery and remediation efforts should focus on strengthening privileged access security to prevent future breaches. Organizations must update security policies, patch vulnerabilities, and conduct security awareness training to reinforce best practices. Regular penetration testing and red team exercises help validate the effectiveness of security controls and identify potential weaknesses before attackers can exploit them. Additionally, continuous monitoring and behavioral analytics should be implemented to detect emerging threats and suspicious privileged account activities in real time.

Lessons learned from each security incident should be documented and used to refine incident response playbooks. By conducting post-incident reviews and analyzing past breaches, organizations can improve their ability to detect, contain, and mitigate future incidents. Cyber threats are constantly evolving, making it essential for organizations to adapt their security strategies, update their PAM configurations, and invest in advanced security technologies to stay ahead of attackers.

A proactive and well-structured incident response and breach containment strategy is essential for minimizing the impact of privileged access security breaches. By implementing strong detection mechanisms, enforcing strict containment measures, conducting forensic investigations, and continuously improving security posture, organizations can effectively protect their most sensitive systems and data from unauthorized access and cyber threats.

Privileged Access in Active Directory Environments

Active Directory (AD) is the backbone of identity and access management for many organizations, providing centralized authentication and authorization across networks. Given its critical role, securing privileged access within AD environments is essential to prevent unauthorized access, privilege escalation, and data breaches. Cyber attackers frequently target AD because compromising privileged accounts within the directory can grant control over an entire organization's IT infrastructure. Implementing robust Privileged Access Management (PAM) strategies in AD environments helps mitigate security risks, enforce least privilege, and ensure compliance with regulatory requirements.

One of the most significant security concerns in AD environments is the overuse of domain administrator accounts. Many organizations grant excessive privileges to users, often allowing IT staff and service accounts to operate with full administrative rights. This practice increases the risk of privilege abuse, insider threats, and lateral movement by attackers who gain a foothold in the network. Enforcing the principle of least privilege (PoLP) is a critical step in securing AD. Instead of using domain administrator accounts for routine tasks, organizations should implement tiered access models that limit administrative privileges based on job responsibilities.

Role-Based Access Control (RBAC) is an effective approach to managing privileged access in AD environments. By defining security groups and assigning permissions based on roles, organizations can ensure that users have only the access necessary for their duties. Implementing Group Policy Objects (GPOs) to enforce security policies across AD-managed endpoints further strengthens access controls. Regular audits of security groups and permissions help identify privilege creep, ensuring that accounts do not accumulate excessive access over time.

Privileged session monitoring is another key component of PAM in AD environments. Administrators must have visibility into privileged user activities to detect suspicious behavior and prevent unauthorized changes to directory services. Implementing session recording and real-time monitoring ensures that all privileged actions are logged and auditable. Security teams can use these logs to analyze user behavior, investigate security incidents, and enforce compliance with internal policies and regulatory standards.

Multi-Factor Authentication (MFA) is an essential security measure for protecting privileged access in AD environments. Traditional username-password authentication is vulnerable to credential theft, phishing, and brute force attacks. Enforcing MFA for administrative accounts significantly reduces the risk of unauthorized access, even if credentials are compromised. Modern PAM solutions integrate with AD to enforce MFA for privileged users accessing domain controllers, remote desktop services, and sensitive applications.

Service accounts present another security challenge in AD environments. These accounts often have elevated privileges and are used by applications, scripts, and automation tools to interact with network resources. Because service account credentials are frequently shared and rarely rotated, they become a high-value target for attackers. Implementing automated credential rotation and vaulting ensures that service account passwords are regularly updated and securely stored. Limiting the scope of service account privileges further reduces the risk of exploitation.

Attackers frequently exploit misconfigurations in AD to escalate privileges and move laterally across networks. Techniques such as Kerberoasting, Pass-the-Hash, and Golden Ticket attacks rely on weaknesses in AD authentication mechanisms. Organizations must regularly assess AD security configurations, apply security patches, and implement advanced threat detection tools to identify and mitigate these risks. Hardening AD environments by disabling unnecessary legacy protocols, enforcing strong password policies, and monitoring authentication logs helps prevent common attack vectors.

Privileged account lifecycle management is crucial for maintaining security in AD environments. Organizations must establish workflows for provisioning, reviewing, and deactivating privileged accounts. Implementing just-in-time (JIT) access further enhances security by granting temporary administrative privileges that expire after a predefined period. This approach minimizes the number of standing privileged accounts and reduces the risk of long-term credential exposure.

Regulatory compliance frameworks such as GDPR, HIPAA, PCI DSS, and NIST require organizations to enforce strict controls over privileged access. PAM solutions integrated with AD help organizations meet compliance requirements by providing audit trails, enforcing least privilege policies, and ensuring continuous monitoring of privileged activities. Generating compliance reports from AD logs and PAM tools simplifies audit processes and demonstrates adherence to security standards.

Incident response planning is an essential aspect of managing privileged access in AD environments. Organizations must develop response protocols for detecting and mitigating unauthorized access attempts. Security teams should conduct regular penetration testing and AD security assessments to identify potential weaknesses. Implementing automated response mechanisms, such as revoking compromised accounts and isolating affected systems, ensures rapid containment of security incidents.

Securing privileged access in Active Directory environments requires a comprehensive approach that includes enforcing least privilege, implementing MFA, monitoring privileged sessions, managing service accounts, and continuously auditing security configurations. By integrating PAM best practices with AD security controls, organizations can effectively protect their IT infrastructure from unauthorized access, insider threats, and cyberattacks.

PAM for Unix/Linux Systems

Privileged Access Management (PAM) is essential for securing Unix and Linux environments, where administrative access to critical systems can lead to significant security risks if not properly managed. These operating systems are widely used in enterprise environments, cloud infrastructure, and development environments, making them a primary target for cyber threats. Properly implementing PAM ensures that privileged access is controlled, monitored, and audited, reducing the risk of unauthorized actions, insider threats, and external attacks.

One of the main challenges in managing privileged access in Unix and Linux systems is the widespread use of the root account. The root user has unrestricted access to all files, configurations, and processes, making it a high-value target for attackers. Organizations must minimize the use of the root account and implement least privilege principles to ensure that users only have the permissions required to perform their tasks. Instead of granting direct root access, administrators should use tools like **sudo**, which allows users to execute specific commands with elevated privileges while maintaining an audit trail of all privileged activities.

Role-Based Access Control (RBAC) is another critical aspect of PAM for Unix and Linux systems. By defining user roles and assigning privileges based on job responsibilities, organizations can limit excessive access and prevent privilege creep. Instead of giving users broad administrative privileges, RBAC ensures that each user can only access the files, processes, and services necessary for their role. Implementing **sudoers** files with granular control over which commands can be executed by specific users further enhances security and accountability.

Session monitoring and logging are key components of PAM in Unix and Linux environments. Administrators must track all privileged activities to detect unauthorized access and potential security incidents. Tools like **auditd** and **syslog** enable organizations to record user sessions, capturing details such as command execution, login attempts, and file modifications. PAM solutions integrate with logging systems to provide real-time alerts and facilitate forensic investigations in case of a security breach.

Multi-Factor Authentication (MFA) is a crucial security measure for privileged accounts in Unix and Linux environments. Traditional password-based authentication is susceptible to brute-force attacks, credential theft, and phishing. Enforcing MFA ensures that privileged users must verify their identity using multiple authentication factors, such as a password combined with a one-time passcode (OTP) or biometric authentication. Many PAM solutions support MFA integration for SSH logins, requiring users to complete additional authentication steps before accessing privileged accounts.

Secure credential management is another essential aspect of PAM in Unix and Linux systems. Many organizations rely on SSH keys for secure remote access, but improper key management can lead to security vulnerabilities. Storing SSH keys in plaintext files, reusing keys across multiple systems, or failing to rotate them regularly increases the risk of unauthorized access. PAM solutions provide secure SSH key management, automating key rotation, enforcing expiration policies, and ensuring that only authorized users can access sensitive systems.

Just-In-Time (JIT) access further strengthens privileged access security in Unix and Linux environments. Instead of granting permanent administrative privileges, JIT access provisions temporary elevated access based on approval workflows. This reduces the attack surface and limits the time frame in which privileged credentials can be exploited. PAM solutions enable administrators to define access policies that require users to request temporary privileges, which are automatically revoked after a predefined period.

Service accounts and automation scripts often require elevated privileges to perform system tasks, such as running cron jobs, managing configurations, and interacting with databases. However, hardcoding passwords or API keys in scripts creates security risks. PAM solutions provide secure vaulting for service account credentials, eliminating the need for static credentials and enforcing strict access controls. Automated password rotation ensures that service account credentials are frequently updated, reducing the risk of credential compromise.

Privileged session isolation is another best practice for Unix and Linux environments. Instead of allowing direct SSH access to critical systems, organizations can use PAM solutions to create secure access gateways that enforce session recording and command filtering. This approach prevents unauthorized users from gaining direct access to privileged systems and ensures that all activities are logged for security auditing.

Compliance with security regulations such as GDPR, PCI DSS, HIPAA, and NIST requires strict controls over privileged access in Unix and Linux systems. PAM solutions help organizations meet these regulatory requirements by enforcing least privilege policies, implementing session monitoring, and maintaining detailed audit logs. Regular security assessments, access reviews, and privilege audits ensure that privileged accounts remain secure and aligned with compliance standards.

Implementing PAM in Unix and Linux environments strengthens security by reducing the risks associated with privileged access.

Enforcing least privilege, securing SSH keys, implementing MFA, monitoring sessions, and automating credential management all contribute to a more secure and compliant infrastructure. Organizations that adopt these best practices can protect their critical systems from unauthorized access, insider threats, and cyberattacks.

Managing Privileged Access in Virtualized Environments

Virtualized environments have become the foundation of modern IT infrastructure, providing organizations with flexibility, scalability, and cost efficiency. However, the increased complexity of virtualization introduces significant security challenges, particularly in managing privileged access. Hypervisors, virtual machines (VMs), and cloud-hosted virtualized infrastructure require strict privileged access controls to prevent unauthorized access, data breaches, and system compromises. A well-structured Privileged Access Management (PAM) strategy ensures that administrators, developers, and automated processes can securely manage virtualized resources while maintaining compliance with security policies and regulatory requirements.

One of the primary risks in virtualized environments is the broad level of access granted to hypervisor administrators. Hypervisors, such as VMware vSphere, Microsoft Hyper-V, and KVM, control the execution of virtual machines and serve as the foundation of the virtualization layer. If an attacker gains privileged access to a hypervisor, they can manipulate virtual machines, extract sensitive data, or disrupt business operations. Implementing the principle of least privilege (PoLP) minimizes this risk by restricting administrative access to only those who require it for specific tasks. Instead of granting full administrative rights to all IT personnel, organizations should use role-based access control (RBAC) to assign granular permissions based on job functions.

Privileged session monitoring plays a crucial role in securing virtualized environments. Administrators frequently access hypervisors, VM consoles, and storage resources to manage workloads. Without proper monitoring, malicious or accidental changes to virtual infrastructure may go undetected. PAM solutions provide real-time session tracking and recording, ensuring that all privileged activities are logged and auditable. Security teams can review these logs to investigate anomalies, detect unauthorized modifications, and enforce compliance requirements.

Credential management is another critical aspect of privileged access in virtualized environments. Many virtualized systems rely on service accounts, API keys, and SSH keys for automation and remote access. If these credentials are not securely managed, attackers can exploit them to gain privileged access. PAM solutions help mitigate this risk by storing credentials in secure vaults, enforcing automated password rotation, and integrating with multi-factor authentication (MFA) mechanisms. By ensuring that privileged credentials are never hardcoded or exposed in scripts, organizations reduce the risk of credential compromise.

The dynamic nature of virtualized environments adds another layer of complexity to privileged access management. Virtual machines, containers, and cloud instances are often created and destroyed rapidly, making it difficult to track and manage privileged accounts. Just-In-Time (JIT) access provisioning is an effective strategy for addressing this challenge. Instead of maintaining persistent privileged accounts, JIT access grants temporary privileges only when needed and automatically revokes them after a predefined period. This approach minimizes the attack surface and reduces the likelihood of unauthorized access.

Virtualized environments frequently integrate with cloud platforms, creating hybrid infrastructures that combine on-premises and cloud-based resources. Managing privileged access across these environments requires a unified PAM strategy that spans both traditional data centers and cloud services. Organizations should integrate PAM solutions with identity and access management (IAM) frameworks used by cloud providers such as AWS, Azure, and Google Cloud. By enforcing consistent access controls across all virtualized resources, organizations can prevent security gaps that arise from managing privileged access in silos.

Third-party vendors and contractors often require privileged access to virtualized environments for maintenance, troubleshooting, or software deployment. Granting unrestricted access to external users increases the risk of security breaches and insider threats. Organizations should enforce strict access approval workflows, implement session recording for vendor activities, and use JIT access to ensure that third-party access is temporary and closely monitored. PAM solutions help enforce these controls by integrating vendor access management features, providing an additional layer of security.

Regulatory compliance is a key consideration when managing privileged access in virtualized environments. Many security frameworks, including GDPR, PCI DSS, HIPAA, and NIST, mandate strict controls over privileged accounts and access monitoring. PAM solutions help organizations meet these compliance requirements by enforcing least privilege policies, generating audit trails, and ensuring that all privileged activities are logged. By aligning virtualization security practices with regulatory standards, organizations reduce the risk of legal and financial penalties associated with non-compliance.

Automation and orchestration further enhance privileged access security in virtualized environments. Organizations can integrate PAM with IT service management (ITSM) platforms and security information and event management (SIEM) systems to automate access requests, enforce security policies, and generate real-time alerts for suspicious privileged activities. By leveraging machine learning and behavioral analytics, PAM solutions can detect anomalies in privileged access patterns, allowing security teams to respond proactively to potential threats.

Organizations must continuously assess and refine their privileged access management strategies to keep pace with evolving threats. Virtualized environments introduce new attack vectors, making it essential to implement robust security controls that prevent unauthorized access while maintaining operational efficiency. By enforcing least privilege access, monitoring privileged sessions, securing credentials, integrating with IAM frameworks, and leveraging automation, organizations can effectively manage privileged access in virtualized environments, reducing security risks and ensuring compliance with industry regulations.

PAM for Mainframe and Legacy Systems

Privileged Access Management (PAM) is critical for securing mainframe and legacy systems, which continue to play a vital role in enterprise IT infrastructures. These systems often handle sensitive data and business-critical applications, making them high-value targets for cyber threats. Unlike modern platforms that support advanced security integrations by default, mainframes and legacy systems were designed in an era where cybersecurity threats were less sophisticated. As a result, implementing PAM in these environments requires specialized strategies to enforce access controls, manage credentials, and monitor privileged activities effectively.

One of the key challenges of managing privileged access in mainframe environments is the reliance on traditional authentication mechanisms. Many mainframes still use basic username-password authentication, which is vulnerable to brute force attacks, credential theft, and insider threats. Integrating modern PAM solutions ensures that privileged accounts leverage strong authentication methods such as multi-factor authentication (MFA), reducing the risk of unauthorized access. Organizations can configure PAM to require additional authentication factors before allowing privileged access to mainframe consoles and administrative interfaces.

Another significant security risk in legacy systems is the widespread use of shared accounts. In many organizations, administrative users access mainframes and legacy applications using generic privileged accounts without individual accountability. This practice makes it difficult to track who performed specific actions and increases the risk of privilege abuse. Implementing PAM introduces secure credential vaulting and session management, ensuring that privileged access is assigned to individual users rather than shared credentials. By enforcing role-based access control (RBAC), organizations can define specific privileges based on job responsibilities, preventing excessive or unnecessary access to critical systems.

Mainframe environments often include batch jobs, automated processes, and service accounts that require elevated privileges to function properly. These accounts are frequently hardcoded with static credentials in scripts, leading to security vulnerabilities if the credentials are not rotated or properly secured. PAM solutions provide automated credential management, ensuring that privileged passwords for batch jobs and service accounts are securely stored and dynamically rotated without disrupting business operations. This reduces the risk of credential compromise while maintaining system functionality.

Session monitoring and auditing play a crucial role in securing privileged access to mainframe and legacy systems. Traditional mainframe interfaces, such as IBM's z/OS or AS/400 systems, often lack built-in session tracking features, making it difficult to detect unauthorized access or privilege misuse. PAM solutions enable real-time session monitoring, recording all privileged activities for forensic analysis and compliance reporting. If suspicious behavior is detected, security teams can respond immediately by terminating sessions, revoking access, or initiating an investigation.

Integrating PAM with legacy systems requires careful planning and adaptation to existing infrastructure constraints. Many legacy applications were not designed to support modern security frameworks, making direct PAM integration complex. Organizations can implement secure access gateways or proxy-based authentication mechanisms to enforce privileged access controls without modifying legacy system code. Using API-based integrations or middleware solutions allows organizations to extend PAM security controls to mainframe environments without disrupting critical operations.

Regulatory compliance is another important factor driving the need for PAM in mainframe and legacy systems. Industries such as finance, healthcare, and government must comply with strict data protection regulations, including GDPR, HIPAA, and PCI DSS. These regulations mandate robust access controls, audit trails, and authentication mechanisms to safeguard sensitive information. PAM helps organizations meet these compliance requirements by enforcing least privilege principles, maintaining detailed access logs, and providing automated reporting for audits.

Many organizations are modernizing their IT environments by migrating workloads from legacy systems to cloud or hybrid infrastructures. However, complete migration is often impractical due to operational dependencies on mainframes. PAM ensures that even as organizations transition to newer technologies, privileged access to legacy systems remains secure. By implementing centralized PAM solutions that manage both modern and legacy environments, organizations can maintain consistent security policies across their entire IT infrastructure.

Securing privileged access in mainframe and legacy environments is essential for preventing unauthorized access, reducing insider threats, and ensuring regulatory compliance. By implementing multi-factor authentication, enforcing credential management, enabling session monitoring, and integrating PAM with existing security frameworks, organizations can strengthen the security of their most critical systems. As cyber threats continue to evolve, maintaining robust privileged access controls in legacy environments is essential for long-term security and operational resilience.

Using PAM with Network Devices and Appliances

Privileged Access Management (PAM) plays a crucial role in securing network devices and appliances, which are often the backbone of an organization's IT infrastructure. Routers, switches, firewalls, load balancers, and other network appliances require privileged access for configuration, maintenance, and troubleshooting. If not properly secured, these devices can become entry points for attackers, allowing them to intercept traffic, disrupt services, or escalate their access within the network. Implementing PAM for network devices ensures that administrative access is tightly controlled, monitored, and aligned with security best practices.

One of the primary challenges in managing privileged access to network devices is the reliance on default or shared administrative accounts. Many network appliances come with factory-default credentials that, if left unchanged, pose a significant security risk. Cybercriminals frequently exploit these well-known default usernames and passwords to gain unauthorized access. PAM solutions enforce strict credential management by storing device credentials in secure vaults, rotating them regularly, and eliminating the need for administrators to manually enter passwords.

Multi-Factor Authentication (MFA) enhances security by requiring additional authentication beyond just a username and password. Many network devices lack built-in MFA support, making it necessary to integrate PAM solutions that enforce MFA through external authentication mechanisms such as RADIUS, TACACS+, or LDAP. By requiring administrators to verify their identity using multiple factors, organizations can reduce the risk of credential-based attacks such as phishing or brute force attempts.

Role-Based Access Control (RBAC) is essential for managing privileged access to network devices. Granting broad administrative privileges to all network engineers increases the risk of accidental misconfigurations or malicious actions. Instead of providing full access to all users, RBAC ensures that administrators only receive the permissions necessary for their job functions. For example, a junior network engineer may have read-only access to device configurations, while a senior administrator may have full control over firewall rules and routing tables.

Just-In-Time (JIT) access further reduces security risks by provisioning temporary privileged access to network devices only when required. Instead of maintaining persistent administrative accounts, JIT access ensures that elevated privileges are granted for a limited period and revoked automatically once the task is completed. This approach minimizes the attack surface and prevents unauthorized users from gaining prolonged access to critical infrastructure.

Privileged session monitoring and recording provide real-time visibility into administrative activities on network devices. Unauthorized configuration changes, suspicious command execution, or unexpected access attempts can indicate a security breach or insider threat. PAM solutions enable organizations to record privileged sessions, generate audit logs, and trigger alerts when anomalies are detected. By integrating PAM with a Security Information and Event Management (SIEM) system, security teams can correlate privileged access events with other security incidents, improving threat detection and incident response.

Network devices often rely on command-line interfaces (CLI) for configuration, making centralized access control a critical security measure. PAM solutions provide secure gateways that mediate privileged access to network appliances, ensuring that all administrative sessions are authenticated, logged, and audited. These gateways prevent direct device access, reducing the risk of credential theft and unauthorized configuration changes.

Third-party vendors and contractors frequently require access to network devices for maintenance, updates, and troubleshooting. Granting unrestricted access to external users increases the likelihood of security breaches and compliance violations. Organizations should implement strict access approval workflows, enforce session monitoring, and apply time-restricted access policies for third-party users. PAM solutions facilitate these controls by providing temporary credentials, tracking vendor activities, and ensuring that all privileged actions are reviewed and audited.

Compliance with security regulations and industry standards requires organizations to enforce strict controls over privileged access to network devices. Regulations such as PCI DSS, GDPR, ISO 27001, and NIST mandate access logging, least privilege enforcement, and periodic access reviews. PAM solutions help organizations achieve compliance by maintaining detailed audit trails, enforcing security policies, and generating compliance reports for regulatory audits.

Automating privileged access workflows reduces administrative overhead while ensuring consistent security enforcement. PAM solutions integrate with network management platforms to automate access provisioning, enforce password rotation, and streamline access approval processes. By eliminating manual credential handling and implementing automated security policies, organizations can improve operational efficiency while strengthening privileged access security.

Securing privileged access to network devices and appliances is a critical aspect of IT security. By implementing PAM solutions that enforce credential management, MFA, RBAC, session monitoring, and automation, organizations can protect their network infrastructure from unauthorized access and security threats. A robust PAM strategy ensures that privileged access to routers, switches, firewalls, and other critical devices is controlled, monitored, and aligned with industry best practices.

Integration with Security Information and Event Management (SIEM)

Integrating Privileged Access Management (PAM) with Security Information and Event Management (SIEM) solutions enhances an organization's security posture by providing real-time monitoring, centralized logging, and advanced threat detection for privileged activities. PAM solutions control and monitor privileged access, while SIEM platforms collect and analyze security data across an enterprise. Together, they create a comprehensive security framework that enables organizations to detect, investigate, and respond to security incidents involving privileged accounts.

Privileged accounts represent a high-risk attack vector because they grant access to critical systems and sensitive data. Attackers often target these accounts to escalate privileges, move laterally through networks, and exfiltrate confidential information. Without proper monitoring, privileged access events may go unnoticed until a breach occurs. Integrating PAM with SIEM allows security teams to correlate privileged access logs with broader security events, identifying anomalies that indicate potential threats.

SIEM platforms aggregate logs from various sources, including firewalls, intrusion detection systems (IDS), endpoint protection tools, and PAM solutions. By integrating PAM data into SIEM, organizations gain visibility into privileged access patterns, such as login attempts, session activities, and policy violations. Correlating privileged access data with other security events helps detect insider threats, compromised accounts, and unauthorized access attempts in real time.

Real-time alerting is a key benefit of PAM-SIEM integration. When unusual privileged access activities occur—such as failed login attempts, privilege escalations, or access from unexpected locations—SIEM platforms generate alerts that allow security teams to investigate and respond immediately. These alerts can trigger automated responses, such as temporarily disabling an account, blocking access to a system, or initiating an incident response workflow. By automating detection and response, organizations can minimize the impact of security incidents involving privileged accounts.

Behavioral analytics enhances privileged access security when PAM and SIEM solutions work together. Modern SIEM platforms use machine learning and artificial intelligence to establish baselines for normal user behavior. When a privileged user deviates from established patterns—such as logging in at an unusual time, accessing an unfamiliar system, or transferring large amounts of data—the SIEM system flags the activity as suspicious. This proactive approach helps organizations detect advanced persistent threats (APTs) and other sophisticated attacks before they cause significant damage.

Compliance and audit readiness improve with PAM-SIEM integration. Many regulatory frameworks, including GDPR, PCI DSS, HIPAA, and ISO 27001, require organizations to enforce strict access controls, maintain audit trails, and detect security incidents involving privileged accounts. By feeding PAM logs into SIEM, organizations create a centralized audit repository that simplifies compliance reporting and forensic investigations. Security teams can generate detailed reports on privileged access activities, demonstrating adherence to regulatory requirements and internal security policies.

Incident response and forensic analysis benefit from PAM-SIEM integration by providing detailed insights into privileged access events.

When a security breach occurs, forensic investigators rely on PAM logs to trace the origin of an attack, determine how an attacker gained access, and identify affected systems. SIEM platforms enhance this process by correlating PAM data with broader security logs, offering a holistic view of an incident. This visibility enables organizations to take corrective actions, such as revoking compromised credentials, applying security patches, or improving access controls.

To maximize the effectiveness of PAM-SIEM integration, organizations must ensure seamless data ingestion and log normalization. PAM solutions generate structured logs detailing privileged access events, which must be formatted correctly for SIEM ingestion. Security teams should configure PAM to send logs via industry-standard protocols such as Syslog or APIs, ensuring that SIEM platforms can process the data efficiently. Proper log categorization and filtering help reduce noise, allowing SIEM systems to focus on high-risk privileged access activities.

Organizations can further enhance security by integrating PAM-SIEM workflows with security orchestration, automation, and response (SOAR) platforms. SOAR solutions automate security tasks, such as triggering incident response actions when a SIEM alert is generated. For example, if a SIEM platform detects an unauthorized privilege escalation, a SOAR playbook can automatically revoke the elevated privileges, notify security teams, and initiate an investigation. This level of automation reduces response times and minimizes the risk of security breaches caused by compromised privileged accounts.

A well-executed PAM-SIEM integration strategy strengthens overall cybersecurity defenses by improving privileged access visibility, enabling proactive threat detection, and facilitating rapid incident response. By combining the access control capabilities of PAM with the analytical power of SIEM, organizations gain a more effective approach to protecting sensitive systems and ensuring regulatory compliance.

Automation and Orchestration in PAM

Automation and orchestration are transforming Privileged Access Management (PAM) by improving security, efficiency, and compliance in managing privileged accounts. Traditional PAM processes often involve manual interventions, such as provisioning privileged access, rotating credentials, and auditing user activities. These manual tasks are time-consuming, prone to human error, and difficult to scale. By implementing automation and orchestration, organizations can streamline PAM operations, enforce security policies consistently, and respond to threats in real time.

Automation in PAM eliminates repetitive administrative tasks, reducing the burden on security teams while ensuring privileged access is managed systematically. One of the most common use cases for automation is credential management. Automated password vaulting and rotation ensure that privileged credentials are securely stored, regularly updated, and never reused. Instead of relying on administrators to manually change passwords, automated PAM solutions enforce strict rotation policies, preventing attackers from exploiting static credentials.

Orchestration takes automation a step further by integrating PAM with other security and IT management tools. By connecting PAM with Security Information and Event Management (SIEM), Security Orchestration, Automation, and Response (SOAR), and Identity and Access Management (IAM) solutions, organizations create a seamless security ecosystem. For example, when a SIEM system detects suspicious activity involving a privileged account, it can trigger an automated response through PAM, such as revoking access, rotating credentials, or launching an investigation.

Just-In-Time (JIT) access is a key feature enabled by PAM automation. Instead of maintaining standing privileged accounts, JIT access provisions temporary administrative rights only when needed. This minimizes the attack surface by ensuring that privileged access is granted for a limited duration and revoked automatically. Automated workflows validate access requests, apply approval processes, and enforce least privilege principles without manual intervention.

Behavioral analytics and artificial intelligence enhance PAM automation by detecting anomalies in privileged access behavior. Machine learning models analyze user activity patterns, identifying deviations such as logins from unusual locations, privilege escalation attempts, or access outside of normal working hours. Automated risk scoring allows organizations to implement adaptive security controls, dynamically adjusting access privileges based on real-time threat assessments.

Orchestration streamlines incident response by enabling coordinated security actions across multiple systems. If a privileged account exhibits signs of compromise, an orchestrated response can automatically isolate the affected account, notify security teams, and trigger forensic analysis. Integrating PAM with endpoint detection and response (EDR) tools ensures that compromised accounts cannot be used to spread attacks within an organization's network.

Compliance enforcement benefits significantly from automation in PAM. Regulatory frameworks such as GDPR, HIPAA, and PCI DSS require strict controls over privileged access, including auditing, logging, and access reviews. Automating these processes ensures that compliance requirements are met consistently. Automated reporting and audit trail generation simplify regulatory audits, providing security teams with real-time insights into privileged activities.

Scaling PAM across cloud, hybrid, and multi-cloud environments requires automation to manage dynamic workloads efficiently. Cloud-native PAM solutions integrate with cloud IAM frameworks, automating privileged access provisioning for virtual machines, containers, and serverless applications. Orchestrating PAM policies across on-premises and cloud environments ensures unified security controls, reducing misconfigurations and security gaps.

As cyber threats continue to evolve, automation and orchestration in PAM provide organizations with the agility needed to protect privileged accounts proactively. By automating credential management, enforcing JIT access, leveraging behavioral analytics, and integrating with security orchestration tools, organizations enhance security while reducing operational complexity. A well-orchestrated

PAM strategy enables faster threat detection, improved compliance, and stronger protection for critical assets.

Machine Identities and Privileged Access

Machine identities play a critical role in modern IT environments, where automation, cloud computing, and interconnected systems rely on non-human entities to authenticate and interact securely. Unlike user identities, which are managed through traditional identity and access management (IAM) systems, machine identities include service accounts, application credentials, API keys, certificates, and cryptographic tokens. Managing privileged access for these machine identities is essential to securing enterprise infrastructure, preventing unauthorized access, and mitigating the risks associated with credential misuse or compromise.

As organizations increase their reliance on cloud services, microservices, and automated workflows, the number of machine identities grows exponentially. Each virtual machine, container, or application component often requires credentials to communicate with other services, access databases, or execute automated processes. Without proper governance, these credentials become difficult to track, leading to security blind spots where privileged access is granted without sufficient oversight. Implementing Privileged Access Management (PAM) for machine identities ensures that these credentials are properly stored, rotated, and restricted based on security best practices.

One of the primary security risks associated with machine identities is the misuse of hardcoded credentials. Many applications, scripts, and infrastructure components rely on embedded passwords or API keys to authenticate with external systems. If these credentials are not encrypted and properly secured, they become a prime target for attackers. Cybercriminals frequently scan repositories, cloud storage, and configuration files for exposed secrets. PAM solutions mitigate this risk by vaulting machine credentials, enforcing access controls, and integrating with secrets management tools to eliminate the need for hardcoded authentication details.

Automated credential rotation is a key security measure for managing machine identities. Unlike user passwords, which are typically updated on a scheduled basis, machine credentials often remain static for extended periods, increasing the risk of unauthorized access. PAM solutions enforce dynamic credential rotation policies that generate and distribute new credentials at regular intervals. This reduces the risk of credential compromise while ensuring seamless authentication for automated processes. Organizations can further enhance security by implementing Just-In-Time (JIT) access for machine identities, granting temporary credentials only when required and revoking them after use.

Secure authentication mechanisms are essential for protecting machine identities. Traditional password-based authentication is insufficient for high-security environments where automation and machine-to-machine (M2M) communication occur at scale. Organizations should implement certificate-based authentication, OAuth tokens, and cryptographic key exchanges to strengthen authentication processes. Using Public Key Infrastructure (PKI) and mutual TLS (mTLS) ensures that only trusted machine identities can access sensitive systems, reducing the risk of unauthorized access.

Privileged session monitoring and logging are crucial for tracking machine identity usage. Unlike human users, machine identities generate a high volume of authentication requests, making it difficult to differentiate between legitimate activity and malicious behavior. PAM solutions provide real-time monitoring, auditing, and anomaly detection capabilities to flag unusual access patterns. If a machine identity suddenly accesses a system outside of normal operational parameters or exhibits signs of credential abuse, security teams can respond proactively by revoking access and investigating potential breaches.

Cloud environments introduce additional complexities in managing machine identities. Cloud workloads, containers, and serverless functions frequently require privileged access to interact with databases, storage services, and third-party APIs. PAM solutions integrate with cloud IAM frameworks to enforce least privilege access policies, ensuring that machine identities have only the permissions necessary for their specific functions. Security teams must continuously audit cloud permissions, remove excessive privileges, and implement fine-grained access controls to minimize the attack surface.

Regulatory compliance mandates strong governance over machine identities and privileged access. Frameworks such as GDPR, HIPAA, PCI DSS, and NIST require organizations to implement robust authentication, encryption, and auditing controls to protect sensitive data. PAM solutions help organizations meet compliance requirements by enforcing access policies, maintaining audit logs, and generating compliance reports. By integrating PAM with security information and event management (SIEM) systems, organizations gain real-time visibility into machine identity activities and potential security incidents.

Third-party integrations and supply chain security further emphasize the importance of machine identity management. Organizations frequently rely on external vendors, cloud providers, and software-as-a-service (SaaS) platforms that require machine-to-machine authentication. PAM solutions ensure that vendor-issued credentials are properly secured, monitored, and restricted to minimize third-party risks. Implementing federated authentication and Zero Trust principles further strengthens access controls by requiring continuous verification of machine identities.

As machine identities continue to proliferate in enterprise environments, organizations must adopt a comprehensive strategy for securing privileged access. Implementing PAM solutions, enforcing credential rotation, leveraging secure authentication mechanisms, and continuously monitoring machine identity activities are critical steps in preventing unauthorized access and reducing security risks. Strengthening governance over machine identities ensures that automated workflows, cloud services, and interconnected systems operate securely while maintaining compliance with industry regulations.

Privileged Access in Internet of Things (IoT)

The Internet of Things (IoT) has revolutionized industries by connecting devices, sensors, and systems to enable real-time data exchange and automation. From smart homes and industrial control systems to healthcare and transportation, IoT devices play a crucial role in modern digital infrastructure. However, the widespread adoption of IoT also introduces significant security risks, particularly in managing privileged access. Unlike traditional IT environments where privileged access is restricted to a limited number of users, IoT ecosystems involve numerous connected devices that require authentication, access controls, and secure communication channels. Without proper Privileged Access Management (PAM), these devices can become entry points for cyberattacks, leading to data breaches, operational disruptions, and regulatory compliance violations.

One of the main challenges in securing privileged access in IoT environments is the sheer scale and diversity of devices. IoT networks often consist of thousands or even millions of connected endpoints, ranging from simple sensors to complex industrial machinery. Many of these devices are deployed in distributed locations with limited security controls, making it difficult to enforce consistent access policies. Unlike traditional IT systems that rely on centralized identity management, IoT devices often operate independently, using hardcoded credentials or weak authentication mechanisms. Attackers exploit these vulnerabilities by targeting default passwords, unsecured APIs, and outdated firmware to gain unauthorized control over IoT systems.

Implementing strong authentication mechanisms is essential to protecting privileged access in IoT environments. Traditional username-password authentication is insufficient for securing IoT devices, as passwords can be easily compromised through brute force attacks or credential leaks. Organizations should adopt certificate-based authentication, public key infrastructure (PKI), and cryptographic tokens to ensure that only authorized devices and users can access privileged functions. Multi-Factor Authentication (MFA) adds an extra layer of security, requiring device administrators to verify their identity using multiple authentication factors before gaining access to IoT management consoles and critical systems.

Role-Based Access Control (RBAC) and Attribute-Based Access Control (ABAC) help enforce least privilege principles in IoT ecosystems. Instead of granting broad administrative access to all users and devices, organizations should implement granular access policies that limit privileges based on specific roles, device attributes, and operational needs. For example, a smart thermostat in a corporate building should only have access to temperature control functions, while an industrial IoT gateway should be restricted to managing factory equipment. By defining access levels based on device type, location, and usage patterns, organizations can minimize the risk of unauthorized access and privilege escalation.

Just-In-Time (JIT) access further enhances IoT security by granting temporary privileges only when needed. IoT devices often require administrative access for software updates, troubleshooting, and configuration changes, but leaving privileged credentials permanently active increases the attack surface. JIT access ensures that administrative privileges are provisioned dynamically and revoked automatically after a predefined period. This approach prevents attackers from exploiting dormant credentials and limits the potential impact of compromised accounts.

Privileged session monitoring and logging play a crucial role in detecting and responding to security incidents in IoT networks. Unlike traditional IT environments where administrators can actively monitor user sessions, IoT devices generate massive volumes of data that make it challenging to track privileged access activities. PAM solutions integrate with Security Information and Event Management (SIEM) platforms to collect, analyze, and correlate privileged access logs across IoT ecosystems. Real-time monitoring enables security teams to identify anomalies, such as unauthorized device access, privilege escalations, and suspicious configuration changes. By leveraging behavioral analytics and machine learning, organizations can detect potential threats before they escalate into full-scale attacks.

IoT devices frequently communicate with cloud services, mobile applications, and third-party platforms, creating additional security risks related to privileged access. Many IoT ecosystems rely on cloud-based management portals for remote administration, exposing privileged credentials to potential interception or misuse.

Organizations must enforce end-to-end encryption, secure API authentication, and robust access controls to protect IoT data exchanges. Implementing Zero Trust principles ensures that every access request, whether from a human user or an IoT device, is verified and validated before granting privileged access.

Firmware security and patch management are critical components of privileged access protection in IoT environments. Many IoT devices operate on outdated firmware with known security vulnerabilities that attackers exploit to gain privileged control. Organizations should establish automated patch management policies that enforce regular firmware updates, security patches, and vulnerability remediation. Secure boot mechanisms and code signing ensure that only trusted firmware versions can run on IoT devices, preventing attackers from injecting malicious code to bypass access controls.

Third-party IoT vendors and service providers often require privileged access to manage devices remotely, adding another layer of security complexity. Organizations must implement strict access approval workflows, enforce vendor access monitoring, and apply time-restricted permissions to prevent excessive privileges. PAM solutions provide centralized access control for third-party integrations, ensuring that external entities follow the same security policies as internal users. Continuous auditing and compliance reporting help organizations maintain visibility into privileged access activities and ensure adherence to regulatory standards such as GDPR, NIST, and ISO 27001.

As IoT adoption continues to grow, securing privileged access remains a top priority for organizations across all industries. By implementing strong authentication mechanisms, enforcing least privilege principles, adopting Just-In-Time access, and continuously monitoring privileged sessions, organizations can mitigate the risks associated with IoT security vulnerabilities. Protecting privileged access in IoT ecosystems ensures that connected devices remain secure, resilient, and compliant with industry best practices.

PAM for Containers and Microservices

Privileged Access Management (PAM) is essential for securing containers and microservices, which have become foundational elements of modern application development and deployment. These technologies offer scalability, flexibility, and automation, but they also introduce unique security challenges. Unlike traditional monolithic applications, containerized environments involve multiple components interacting dynamically, often requiring privileged access to function properly. Without proper PAM controls, mismanaged privileges can lead to unauthorized access, lateral movement, and potential exploitation of sensitive data.

One of the primary challenges in container security is the widespread use of root privileges. Many containerized applications run as root by default, exposing the underlying host system to security risks. If an attacker compromises a privileged container, they can potentially gain access to the entire host or escalate privileges across multiple services. Enforcing least privilege is critical in containerized environments. Organizations should implement policies that prevent containers from running with root privileges unless absolutely necessary, and use user namespaces to isolate processes from the host system.

Managing secrets such as API keys, credentials, and encryption keys is another significant aspect of PAM for containers and microservices. These secrets are often needed for service-to-service communication, database access, and integration with external systems. Hardcoded credentials in container images or environment variables create serious security vulnerabilities. Attackers who gain access to a running container can easily extract these secrets, leading to unauthorized access. Using a secure secrets management solution integrated with PAM ensures that sensitive credentials are stored securely, retrieved only when needed, and rotated regularly.

Container orchestration platforms, such as Kubernetes, introduce additional complexities in managing privileged access. Kubernetes clusters consist of multiple components, including the control plane, worker nodes, and containerized workloads, all of which require careful access management. Kubernetes role-based access control (RBAC) helps define granular permissions for different users, services, and processes. By integrating PAM with Kubernetes RBAC, organizations can enforce least privilege principles, monitor privileged activities, and prevent excessive permissions from being assigned unintentionally.

Just-In-Time (JIT) access is particularly effective in securing containerized environments. Instead of granting persistent administrative privileges to developers or automation tools, JIT access provisions temporary access based on predefined approval workflows. For example, a developer needing access to a production container can request temporary elevated privileges, which are automatically revoked once the session ends. This approach minimizes the risk of privilege abuse and ensures that access is granted only when necessary.

Privileged session monitoring and auditing are crucial for tracking access to containerized environments. Because microservices often communicate dynamically, it is essential to have visibility into who accessed what, when, and for what purpose. PAM solutions integrated with log aggregation and Security Information and Event Management (SIEM) systems provide real-time monitoring of privileged activities, allowing security teams to detect anomalies, unauthorized access attempts, and potential breaches.

Automated workload identity management is another key component of PAM in containerized environments. Unlike traditional applications where authentication is user-centric, containerized workloads need their own identities to securely interact with each other. Using workload identities and implementing strong authentication mechanisms, such as mutual TLS (mTLS) or OAuth-based service authentication, ensures that only authorized containers can communicate with critical services.

Securing privileged access in DevOps pipelines is also critical, as containers are frequently built, tested, and deployed through automated CI/CD processes. If CI/CD tools have excessive privileges, a compromised pipeline can lead to a full-scale breach. Implementing PAM within DevOps workflows ensures that CI/CD tools use least privilege access, secrets are managed securely, and any privileged actions performed by automated scripts are logged and monitored.

Compliance and regulatory requirements also apply to containerized environments. Regulations such as GDPR, PCI DSS, and HIPAA mandate strict access controls, auditing, and privileged session monitoring. PAM solutions help organizations meet these compliance requirements by enforcing access policies, generating audit trails, and providing real-time alerts for suspicious privileged activities.

By integrating PAM with container orchestration platforms, enforcing least privilege, securing secrets, and implementing JIT access, organizations can effectively manage privileged access in containerized and microservices-based environments. These security measures reduce the attack surface, prevent unauthorized access, and ensure that only trusted entities can interact with sensitive workloads, maintaining a strong security posture in dynamic cloud-native architectures.

Emerging Trends in Privileged Access Management

Privileged Access Management (PAM) continues to evolve in response to the increasing sophistication of cyber threats, the shift to cloud computing, and the expansion of digital transformation initiatives. As organizations modernize their IT infrastructures, they must adapt their PAM strategies to address new security challenges, regulatory requirements, and operational complexities. Emerging trends in PAM focus on automation, Zero Trust architecture, artificial intelligence, cloud-native security, and machine identity management, each playing a crucial role in enhancing privileged access security.

The adoption of Zero Trust principles is reshaping the way organizations manage privileged access. Traditional security models relied on network perimeters to protect sensitive assets, but modern environments require a more dynamic approach. Zero Trust enforces the principle of "never trust, always verify," requiring continuous authentication and authorization for every privileged access request.

PAM solutions are integrating with identity and access management (IAM) systems to enforce Zero Trust by validating user identities, verifying device security posture, and applying contextual access controls.

Artificial intelligence (AI) and machine learning (ML) are transforming PAM by enabling intelligent threat detection and response. Behavioral analytics powered by AI help identify anomalies in privileged user activity, detecting unusual access patterns that may indicate insider threats or compromised credentials. Instead of relying solely on predefined rules, AI-driven PAM solutions dynamically adapt to emerging threats, triggering automated security responses such as session termination, privilege revocation, or real-time alerts to security teams.

Cloud-native PAM is becoming a necessity as organizations migrate workloads to cloud platforms. Traditional PAM solutions were designed for on-premises environments, but modern enterprises operate in multi-cloud and hybrid cloud ecosystems. Cloud-native PAM solutions offer seamless integration with cloud IAM frameworks, enforcing least privilege access policies across cloud workloads, virtual machines, and containerized applications. These solutions provide just-in-time (JIT) access provisioning, ephemeral credential management, and automated risk assessment to secure privileged access in cloud environments.

The rise of machine identities is driving the need for enhanced credential management and authentication mechanisms. As organizations embrace automation, DevOps, and Internet of Things (IoT) technologies, the number of non-human identities requiring privileged access is growing exponentially. PAM solutions are evolving to manage machine identities by enforcing certificate-based authentication, API key rotation, and secure vaulting for application credentials. Managing machine identities effectively reduces the risk of credential sprawl and unauthorized system access.

Privileged access security is also shifting toward continuous adaptive trust. Instead of granting static, long-term privileges, modern PAM strategies focus on adaptive access control, where access rights are dynamically adjusted based on real-time risk assessments. Factors such as user behavior, device compliance, location, and historical activity influence privilege elevation decisions. This approach minimizes the attack surface while maintaining operational flexibility for administrators and service accounts.

The integration of PAM with broader security ecosystems is enhancing threat detection and response capabilities. PAM solutions now integrate with Security Information and Event Management (SIEM), Security Orchestration, Automation, and Response (SOAR), and Endpoint Detection and Response (EDR) platforms. This interconnected security approach enables organizations to correlate privileged access events with broader security incidents, providing deeper visibility into potential threats. Automated workflows facilitate rapid incident response, allowing security teams to revoke access, isolate compromised accounts, and contain breaches before they escalate.

Regulatory compliance requirements continue to shape PAM advancements. Organizations must adhere to stringent data protection laws such as GDPR, PCI DSS, HIPAA, and NIST guidelines, all of which emphasize strict access controls, continuous monitoring, and audit logging for privileged activities. Emerging PAM solutions incorporate automated compliance reporting, real-time audit trails, and policy enforcement to help organizations meet regulatory obligations without disrupting business operations.

As the cybersecurity landscape evolves, PAM solutions must continuously adapt to address emerging threats and operational challenges. The convergence of Zero Trust, AI-driven threat detection, cloud-native security, and machine identity management is shaping the future of privileged access security. Organizations that embrace these innovations will strengthen their security posture, reduce the risk of privileged credential compromise, and enhance their ability to manage privileged access in complex, dynamic IT environments.

Evaluating and Selecting PAM Solutions

Choosing the right Privileged Access Management (PAM) solution is a critical decision for organizations seeking to secure privileged credentials, enforce least privilege policies, and maintain compliance with regulatory requirements. With a growing number of PAM vendors offering different capabilities, organizations must carefully evaluate solutions based on security effectiveness, scalability, integration capabilities, and operational efficiency. A well-selected PAM solution enhances security while minimizing administrative overhead and ensuring a seamless user experience.

One of the first factors to consider when evaluating PAM solutions is core functionality. A comprehensive PAM solution should include privileged account discovery, credential vaulting, automated password rotation, session monitoring, and just-in-time (JIT) access provisioning. Organizations should assess whether the PAM tool can effectively identify and secure all privileged accounts across their IT infrastructure, including on-premises servers, cloud environments, network devices, and third-party integrations.

Security and compliance requirements play a significant role in PAM selection. Organizations operating in regulated industries such as finance, healthcare, and government must ensure that the chosen PAM solution meets compliance standards like GDPR, HIPAA, PCI DSS, and NIST. Features such as automated audit logging, role-based access control (RBAC), multi-factor authentication (MFA), and real-time session monitoring help organizations demonstrate compliance and maintain a strong security posture.

Scalability is another key consideration. As organizations grow and adopt new technologies, their privileged access requirements evolve. A PAM solution should be capable of scaling with the organization's needs, supporting hybrid IT environments, multi-cloud deployments, and remote workforces. Cloud-native PAM solutions offer greater flexibility and scalability, allowing organizations to secure privileged access across distributed environments without the limitations of traditional on-premises deployments.

Integration with existing IT and security ecosystems is crucial for a PAM solution's effectiveness. Organizations should evaluate whether the solution can integrate with identity and access management (IAM) platforms, security information and event management (SIEM) systems, endpoint protection solutions, and IT service management (ITSM) tools. Seamless integration enhances visibility, streamlines security operations, and enables automated responses to privileged access threats.

User experience and operational efficiency are also important factors in PAM selection. A well-designed PAM solution should balance security with usability, ensuring that administrators, developers, and IT teams can access privileged resources efficiently while maintaining security best practices. Features such as single sign-on (SSO), self-service credential retrieval, and adaptive access controls help improve usability without compromising security.

Cost considerations play a role in PAM evaluation. Organizations must assess the total cost of ownership (TCO), including licensing fees, implementation costs, maintenance expenses, and training requirements. Some vendors offer subscription-based pricing models, while others provide on-premises deployments with perpetual licenses. Comparing pricing structures and aligning them with budgetary constraints helps organizations select a PAM solution that delivers the best value.

Organizations should conduct proof-of-concept (PoC) testing before finalizing their PAM selection. A PoC allows security teams to evaluate the solution's capabilities in a controlled environment, testing key functionalities such as credential management, session monitoring, and privilege escalation controls. By gathering feedback from IT administrators and end-users, organizations can determine whether the solution meets their security requirements and operational needs.

Vendor reputation and support services should also be considered. Established PAM vendors with a strong track record of innovation, customer support, and security expertise provide greater assurance of long-term reliability. Organizations should evaluate vendor support offerings, including response times, training resources, and service-level agreements (SLAs), to ensure that they receive adequate assistance during deployment and ongoing operations.

Selecting the right PAM solution requires a strategic approach that aligns with organizational security goals, compliance requirements, and IT infrastructure needs. By assessing functionality, scalability, integration capabilities, user experience, and vendor reputation, organizations can implement a PAM solution that enhances privileged access security while supporting business agility and operational efficiency.

Deploying and Scaling a PAM Solution

Deploying and scaling a Privileged Access Management (PAM) solution is a crucial step in securing an organization's most sensitive accounts, systems, and data. As cyber threats continue to evolve, ensuring that privileged access is properly managed, monitored, and protected becomes a top priority for businesses of all sizes. A well-planned PAM deployment enables organizations to enforce least privilege access, implement robust authentication mechanisms, and maintain compliance with security regulations while scaling the solution to meet growing operational needs.

The first phase of deploying a PAM solution involves conducting a comprehensive assessment of the organization's privileged access landscape. This includes identifying all privileged accounts, service accounts, administrative users, and machine identities that require access control. Many organizations underestimate the number of privileged accounts within their environment, leading to security gaps. A thorough discovery process ensures that all high-risk access points are identified and addressed during implementation.

Once the privileged accounts are mapped, organizations must define policies and controls based on security best practices. Implementing role-based access control (RBAC) and just-in-time (JIT) privilege escalation helps enforce least privilege principles while reducing the attack surface. Defining access approval workflows ensures that only authorized users can obtain privileged access, reducing the risk of insider threats and credential misuse.

Integration with existing IT infrastructure is a key consideration in PAM deployment. Organizations must ensure that their PAM solution integrates seamlessly with identity and access management (IAM) platforms, directory services such as Active Directory (AD), and cloud environments. Many modern PAM solutions support hybrid deployments, enabling organizations to manage privileged access across on-premises data centers, multi-cloud environments, and SaaS applications. Proper integration ensures that PAM policies are consistently enforced across all systems.

Authentication mechanisms play a critical role in securing privileged access. Multi-factor authentication (MFA) should be mandated for all privileged accounts, reducing the risk of credential-based attacks. Secure credential storage through a centralized password vault ensures that privileged passwords are encrypted, rotated regularly, and never exposed to users. By eliminating hardcoded credentials and enforcing automated password management, organizations can significantly enhance security.

Scaling a PAM solution requires careful planning to accommodate organizational growth, increasing workloads, and expanding IT environments. A scalable PAM architecture must support additional users, workloads, and privileged accounts without degrading performance. Cloud-native PAM solutions provide elastic scalability, allowing organizations to dynamically adjust resources based on demand. For on-premises deployments, organizations must ensure that PAM infrastructure can handle increased authentication requests and session monitoring as privileged access requirements grow.

Privileged session monitoring and auditing are essential for maintaining visibility into administrative activities. As organizations scale their PAM implementation, real-time session recording, anomaly detection, and automated alerting become critical components of security operations. SIEM and SOAR integrations enable security teams to correlate PAM events with broader security incidents, improving threat detection and incident response.

Ensuring high availability and resilience is another important aspect of scaling a PAM solution. Redundant architectures, load balancing, and failover mechanisms help maintain uninterrupted access to PAM services in case of system failures. For global enterprises, deploying PAM across multiple geographic locations with regional data centers ensures compliance with data sovereignty regulations while maintaining performance for distributed teams.

User training and adoption are key to the successful deployment and scaling of PAM. Administrators, IT teams, and end users must be educated on PAM policies, security best practices, and access request workflows. Continuous security awareness programs help reinforce the importance of privileged access security and reduce the likelihood of misconfigurations or policy violations.

Regular audits and continuous improvement ensure that the PAM solution remains effective as the organization evolves. Conducting periodic access reviews, privilege audits, and security assessments helps identify gaps and optimize PAM policies. Organizations should adapt their PAM strategy to align with emerging threats, regulatory changes, and evolving IT landscapes, ensuring that privileged access remains secure at all times.

Deploying and scaling a PAM solution requires a strategic approach that balances security, usability, and operational efficiency. By implementing strong access controls, integrating with existing IT environments, enforcing authentication mechanisms, and ensuring scalability, organizations can effectively protect privileged access while maintaining compliance and business continuity. A well-executed PAM deployment strengthens overall cybersecurity resilience, reducing the risk of privileged account exploitation and unauthorized access.

Best Practices for PAM Implementation

Implementing Privileged Access Management (PAM) is a critical step in securing an organization's IT infrastructure, reducing insider threats, and protecting sensitive data. A well-structured PAM implementation helps enforce least privilege access, monitor privileged sessions, and maintain compliance with regulatory requirements. Organizations that follow best practices in PAM implementation can effectively manage privileged accounts, mitigate security risks, and ensure that only authorized users have access to critical systems.

One of the foundational best practices for PAM implementation is conducting a comprehensive discovery of all privileged accounts across the organization. Many organizations have unmanaged or orphaned privileged accounts that pose security risks if left unchecked. Identifying and cataloging all administrative accounts, service accounts, API keys, and shared credentials ensures that no privileged access goes unnoticed. PAM solutions provide automated discovery tools that help security teams locate and secure privileged accounts across on-premises, cloud, and hybrid environments.

Enforcing the principle of least privilege (PoLP) is essential for minimizing the risks associated with privileged access. Instead of granting broad administrative privileges, organizations should restrict access based on job roles and specific tasks. Role-Based Access Control (RBAC) and Attribute-Based Access Control (ABAC) help ensure that users receive only the permissions necessary to perform their duties. Implementing Just-In-Time (JIT) access further enhances security by granting temporary privileges when needed and revoking them automatically after use.

Credential management is a key aspect of PAM implementation. Hardcoded passwords, shared credentials, and static administrative accounts create significant security vulnerabilities. Organizations should use secure vaulting solutions to store privileged credentials, enforce automated password rotation, and eliminate the need for users to manually enter passwords. Multi-Factor Authentication (MFA) adds an additional layer of security, ensuring that privileged users must verify their identity before accessing sensitive systems.

Monitoring and auditing privileged sessions help organizations detect and respond to suspicious activities in real time. PAM solutions offer session recording, keystroke logging, and behavioral analytics to track privileged access. Security teams can review session logs to identify anomalies, investigate unauthorized access attempts, and ensure compliance with security policies. Integrating PAM with Security Information and Event Management (SIEM) systems enhances visibility by correlating privileged access events with broader security incidents.

Organizations should also implement secure access gateways to control and mediate privileged access. Instead of allowing direct access to critical systems, PAM solutions provide proxy-based access, enforcing authentication and authorization policies before granting entry. This approach reduces the risk of credential theft, prevents lateral movement by attackers, and ensures that all privileged activities are logged for auditing purposes.

Regular access reviews and privilege audits are necessary to maintain a secure PAM program. Over time, users may accumulate unnecessary privileges, leading to privilege creep. Periodic access reviews help security teams identify redundant accounts, revoke excessive permissions, and ensure that all privileged access aligns with business needs. Automated reporting tools streamline this process, providing administrators with insights into privileged account usage and compliance status.

Securing machine identities is becoming increasingly important in PAM implementation. Service accounts, application credentials, and API keys require privileged access to interact with IT systems, yet they often lack proper governance. Organizations should enforce machine identity management policies, implement certificate-based authentication, and regularly rotate credentials for automated processes. Protecting machine identities helps prevent unauthorized system access and reduces the risk of credential compromise.

Training and awareness programs ensure that employees understand the importance of privileged access security. Many security breaches occur due to human error, such as weak password practices or accidental privilege misuse. Educating IT administrators, developers, and end-users about PAM policies, security best practices, and compliance requirements strengthens the overall security culture within an organization.

Maintaining a PAM program requires continuous monitoring, updates, and improvements. Cyber threats and regulatory requirements evolve over time, making it essential for organizations to regularly assess their PAM strategies, update security policies, and adopt new technologies to address emerging risks. By following best practices in PAM implementation, organizations can secure privileged access, prevent unauthorized activities, and protect their most critical assets.

Maintaining and Evolving Your PAM Program

Implementing a Privileged Access Management (PAM) program is not a one-time effort but an ongoing process that requires continuous monitoring, refinement, and adaptation to evolving security threats and business needs. As organizations expand their IT infrastructure, adopt new technologies, and respond to emerging cyber risks, PAM programs must evolve to remain effective. Regularly updating privileged access policies, incorporating new security controls, and aligning with compliance requirements ensures that privileged access remains secure while supporting operational efficiency.

One of the most critical aspects of maintaining a PAM program is conducting continuous access reviews. Over time, users, applications, and automated processes may accumulate unnecessary privileges, leading to privilege creep. Periodic access reviews help identify accounts with excessive permissions, ensuring that privileges are revoked or adjusted according to business needs. Automating this process with access certification workflows allows security teams to streamline privilege management, reducing human errors and improving accountability.

Privileged credentials must be managed dynamically to prevent unauthorized access and reduce the risk of credential-based attacks. Automated password rotation ensures that privileged credentials are regularly updated and never remain static for extended periods. Enforcing strong authentication mechanisms, such as Multi-Factor Authentication (MFA) and passwordless authentication, further enhances security by ensuring that only verified users can access critical systems. Monitoring authentication logs for anomalies helps detect compromised accounts before they can be exploited.

As organizations adopt cloud services, containerized applications, and DevOps methodologies, PAM strategies must extend beyond traditional on-premises environments. Cloud-native PAM solutions provide visibility into privileged access across multi-cloud platforms, ensuring that administrators, developers, and automated processes follow least privilege principles. Implementing Just-In-Time (JIT) access controls in cloud environments prevents long-standing privileged credentials from being misused.

Privileged session monitoring and behavioral analytics play a crucial role in evolving a PAM program. By continuously tracking privileged user activity and using machine learning models to detect deviations from normal behavior, organizations can proactively identify insider threats and potential security breaches. Integrating PAM with Security Information and Event Management (SIEM) platforms and Security Orchestration, Automation, and Response (SOAR) tools enables automated responses to suspicious activities, such as revoking access or isolating compromised accounts.

Regulatory compliance requirements frequently change, necessitating adjustments to PAM policies. Organizations must stay updated on security regulations such as GDPR, HIPAA, PCI DSS, and NIST guidelines to ensure ongoing compliance. Regular internal audits, policy reviews, and security assessments help identify gaps in PAM implementation and provide opportunities to enhance security controls. Generating detailed reports on privileged access activities allows organizations to demonstrate compliance to auditors and regulators.

User education and awareness remain essential for maintaining a strong PAM program. IT administrators, developers, and security teams must be regularly trained on privileged access policies, best practices, and potential threats. Ongoing security awareness programs ensure that users understand the importance of following PAM guidelines and reduce the likelihood of misconfigurations or policy violations.

As new attack techniques emerge, PAM programs must incorporate advanced security measures, such as Zero Trust principles, biometric authentication, and AI-driven threat detection. Organizations should continuously evaluate their PAM solutions, explore new security technologies, and refine their strategies to mitigate evolving threats. A well-maintained and adaptive PAM program strengthens an organization's cybersecurity posture, reducing the risk of privileged access abuse and ensuring that critical assets remain protected.

Training and Awareness for PAM Stakeholders

Effective Privileged Access Management (PAM) requires more than just technology; it demands a well-informed workforce that understands the importance of securing privileged accounts. Training and awareness programs ensure that all stakeholders, from IT administrators to business executives, comprehend their role in protecting privileged access. Without proper education, even the most advanced PAM solutions can fail due to misconfigurations, improper usage, or lack of enforcement. By implementing a structured training program, organizations can significantly reduce security risks and enhance compliance with regulatory requirements.

One of the most important aspects of PAM training is ensuring that IT administrators and security personnel are fully equipped to manage privileged accounts securely. These individuals are responsible for configuring, maintaining, and monitoring PAM solutions, making it essential that they understand best practices for least privilege access, credential vaulting, session monitoring, and access review processes. They should receive hands-on training on how to use PAM tools effectively, interpret access logs, and respond to security incidents related to privileged accounts.

End-user training is equally important, particularly for employees who have access to sensitive systems. While they may not be directly responsible for PAM configuration, they must understand how privileged access policies affect their daily operations. Users should be educated on secure authentication practices, the dangers of sharing credentials, and the importance of multi-factor authentication (MFA). Awareness campaigns can help reinforce security policies, ensuring that privileged accounts are not misused or inadvertently exposed to risk.

Training programs must also address executive leadership, as senior management plays a key role in driving PAM initiatives and ensuring compliance. Executives should be aware of the financial, operational, and reputational risks associated with privileged account breaches. Their training should focus on the strategic importance of PAM, regulatory obligations, and the impact of security incidents on business continuity. By securing executive buy-in, organizations can ensure that PAM initiatives receive the necessary resources and prioritization.

Third-party vendors and contractors who require privileged access to organizational systems must also be included in PAM training efforts. External users often pose a significant security risk, as they may not be fully aware of an organization's internal security policies. Before granting privileged access, organizations should require vendors to complete security training, adhere to PAM guidelines, and follow strict access approval workflows. Implementing least privilege access and session monitoring further reduces risks associated with third-party access.

Interactive training methods such as simulations, phishing awareness campaigns, and hands-on workshops are highly effective in reinforcing PAM concepts. Organizations should conduct regular security drills to test employees' responses to simulated privileged access threats, such as credential compromise or unauthorized · privilege escalation attempts. These exercises help stakeholders recognize potential security risks and respond appropriately in real-world scenarios.

Continuous learning and refresher training sessions should be an integral part of the PAM program. Cyber threats evolve constantly, requiring organizations to update their security policies and train employees accordingly. Periodic assessments, knowledge checks, and awareness campaigns ensure that stakeholders remain informed about the latest PAM best practices, compliance requirements, and emerging attack techniques targeting privileged accounts.

By fostering a strong security culture and emphasizing the importance of privileged access management, organizations can significantly enhance their overall cybersecurity posture. Training and awareness programs empower stakeholders to make informed decisions, reduce the risk of human error, and ensure that PAM policies are effectively implemented across the organization.

Advanced Analytics and Machine Learning in PAM

Advanced Analytics and Machine Learning in PAM

Privileged Access Management (PAM) plays a crucial role in securing critical systems by enforcing strict controls over privileged accounts. As cyber threats grow in complexity, organizations must adopt advanced analytics and machine learning (ML) to enhance their PAM capabilities. Traditional rule-based security models are no longer sufficient to detect sophisticated attacks, making AI-driven solutions essential for real-time threat detection, risk assessment, and adaptive access controls.

Machine learning enhances PAM by identifying behavioral anomalies in privileged user activities. Instead of relying solely on predefined rules, ML models analyze historical access patterns to establish a baseline of normal behavior. When a privileged user deviates from expected actions—such as logging in from an unusual location, accessing unfamiliar systems, or performing privilege escalations at odd hours—the system can flag the activity as suspicious. Unlike static policies, ML continuously adapts to changing behavior, improving the accuracy of threat detection while reducing false positives.

Predictive analytics in PAM helps organizations proactively mitigate risks before security incidents occur. By analyzing past access behaviors, login attempts, and privilege usage trends, ML algorithms can predict potential security threats. For example, if an administrator frequently accesses a set of systems but suddenly requests access to a high-risk server they have never used before, predictive analytics can assess the risk and enforce additional verification measures, such as multi-factor authentication (MFA) or manual approval workflows.

Automated anomaly detection streamlines security operations by reducing the burden on IT and security teams. Traditional log analysis requires manual correlation of vast amounts of privileged access data, making it difficult to detect subtle threats in real time. ML-driven PAM solutions automatically sift through privileged access logs, identify unusual patterns, and escalate critical threats to security analysts. This automation improves response times, enabling faster mitigation of potential breaches.

Adaptive access control is another key benefit of integrating ML into PAM. Instead of granting static privileges, ML-driven systems evaluate risk in real time and dynamically adjust access permissions. If a privileged user exhibits unusual behavior, the system can enforce just-in-time (JIT) access, limit session duration, or revoke privileges until further verification is performed. This real-time decision-making enhances security without disrupting business operations.

Machine learning also improves the accuracy of privileged session monitoring. PAM solutions that integrate ML-based session analytics can analyze command-line inputs, keystrokes, and behavioral patterns during privileged sessions. If a user suddenly executes commands unrelated to their normal workflow, the system can generate alerts, initiate session recording, or terminate the session automatically. This level of granular monitoring helps prevent insider threats and unauthorized activities.

The integration of AI and ML with PAM extends beyond user access to include machine identities and automated processes. Many organizations use service accounts, APIs, and robotic process automation (RPA) bots that require privileged access. ML-driven PAM solutions help monitor machine identity behaviors, detect credential misuse, and enforce least privilege access policies dynamically. As machine identities grow in number, AI-powered analytics provide the scalability needed to secure these non-human accounts effectively.

Compliance and auditing are also enhanced with ML-based PAM solutions. Regulatory frameworks such as GDPR, HIPAA, and PCI DSS require organizations to maintain detailed logs of privileged access activities. ML automates compliance reporting by generating real-time risk assessments, identifying policy violations, and prioritizing audit findings. This reduces the manual effort required for compliance management while ensuring that security policies align with regulatory standards.

Organizations adopting ML-driven PAM solutions must also address challenges such as model accuracy, data privacy, and integration with existing security frameworks. Training ML models requires high-quality access data to ensure reliable predictions. Additionally, AI-driven security decisions should be explainable and transparent to avoid unintended access denials or privilege escalations.

The future of PAM lies in leveraging AI and ML to provide intelligent, adaptive security controls. As cyber threats continue to evolve, organizations must integrate advanced analytics into their privileged access strategies. By using machine learning to detect anomalies, predict risks, and enforce real-time access policies, organizations can strengthen their defenses against insider threats, credential-based attacks, and unauthorized privilege escalations.

Threat Intelligence and Privileged Access

Threat intelligence plays a critical role in securing privileged access by providing organizations with insights into emerging cyber threats, attack techniques, and potential vulnerabilities. Privileged accounts are among the most targeted assets in an enterprise, as they grant extensive access to critical systems and sensitive data. Cybercriminals, insider threats, and nation-state actors continuously seek ways to compromise privileged credentials, allowing them to escalate privileges, move laterally within networks, and exfiltrate valuable information. By integrating threat intelligence with Privileged Access Management (PAM), organizations can proactively detect, mitigate, and respond to security threats before they lead to major breaches.

Understanding the threat landscape is the first step in enhancing privileged access security. Threat intelligence provides real-time data on attack patterns, malware campaigns, and known vulnerabilities affecting privileged accounts. Indicators of Compromise (IoCs), such as suspicious login attempts, privilege escalation activities, and anomalous access requests, can help security teams identify potential threats before they escalate. Integrating PAM with threat intelligence feeds enables automated correlation between privileged access events and known cyber threats, allowing organizations to block unauthorized access attempts and prevent privilege abuse.

Credential theft is one of the most common tactics used by attackers to gain unauthorized privileged access. Advanced persistent threats (APTs), ransomware groups, and insider threats often rely on stolen credentials to bypass traditional security controls. Threat intelligence can help organizations identify compromised credentials by monitoring dark web forums, underground marketplaces, and leaked database repositories. By leveraging this intelligence, PAM solutions can enforce immediate credential rotation, revoke compromised accounts, and prevent attackers from exploiting stolen access rights.

Behavioral analytics and machine learning enhance threat intelligence by identifying deviations from normal privileged user behavior. Instead of relying solely on static rules, modern PAM solutions use AI-driven anomaly detection to flag suspicious privileged activities. For example, if an administrator logs in from an unusual location, accesses a sensitive system at an irregular time, or initiates mass data transfers, PAM can trigger automated security responses, such as requiring multi-factor authentication (MFA), limiting session privileges, or alerting security teams for further investigation.

Threat intelligence also plays a crucial role in defending against zero-day attacks and emerging threats targeting privileged access. Traditional security measures often fail to detect novel attack techniques, as they rely on known signatures and predefined rules. By incorporating threat intelligence from industry sources, government agencies, and cybersecurity research groups, PAM solutions can adapt to new attack vectors, implement proactive controls, and strengthen security policies to mitigate potential risks.

Privileged session monitoring is another key component of integrating threat intelligence with PAM. Organizations can use real-time monitoring tools to detect suspicious command executions, unauthorized privilege escalations, and unusual network activity associated with privileged accounts. Correlating this data with external threat intelligence sources helps security teams determine whether an ongoing privileged session is part of a larger attack campaign. Automated response mechanisms, such as terminating suspicious sessions or isolating affected endpoints, help prevent attackers from exploiting privileged access.

Threat intelligence-driven access controls help organizations enforce dynamic security policies based on real-time risk assessments. Instead of applying static privilege rules, adaptive access controls adjust permissions based on contextual threat data. For instance, if a specific geographic region experiences a surge in cyberattacks, PAM can automatically restrict privileged access from that location or require additional authentication steps. By leveraging real-time threat intelligence, organizations can minimize the attack surface while maintaining operational flexibility.

Incident response and forensic investigations benefit significantly from integrating PAM with threat intelligence. When a security breach occurs, threat intelligence provides valuable insights into the tactics, techniques, and procedures (TTPs) used by attackers. By analyzing privileged access logs and correlating them with external threat data, security teams can identify the root cause of an incident, assess the extent of compromise, and implement corrective actions to prevent future attacks. Automated threat intelligence sharing between PAM, Security Information and Event Management (SIEM), and Security Orchestration, Automation, and Response (SOAR) platforms enhances incident response efficiency.

Continuous threat intelligence updates ensure that PAM strategies remain effective against evolving cyber threats. Attackers constantly refine their methods to bypass security controls, making it essential for organizations to stay ahead of emerging risks. Regularly updating PAM configurations, refining access policies, and incorporating new threat intelligence sources help organizations strengthen their privileged access security posture.

Threat intelligence is a powerful tool for enhancing privileged access security by providing real-time insights into cyber threats, identifying compromised credentials, detecting anomalous behavior, and enabling adaptive access controls. By integrating PAM with threat intelligence feeds, behavioral analytics, and automated response mechanisms, organizations can proactively defend against privilege-based attacks, reduce security risks, and improve their overall cybersecurity resilience.

Case Studies in PAM Success and Failures

Privileged Access Management (PAM) is a crucial security framework that protects organizations from unauthorized access, insider threats, and credential-based cyberattacks. While many organizations successfully implement PAM solutions to strengthen security, others face challenges that lead to security failures. Examining real-world case studies of both successful PAM deployments and notable failures provides valuable insights into best practices and potential pitfalls.

One example of a successful PAM implementation comes from a global financial institution that was struggling with excessive privileged accounts and poor credential management. The organization had thousands of administrative accounts with static passwords, increasing the risk of credential theft. After experiencing a security audit failure, the company implemented a PAM solution with automated credential rotation, multi-factor authentication (MFA), and real-time session monitoring. By integrating PAM with their Security Information and Event Management (SIEM) system, they gained greater visibility into privileged activities. As a result, they reduced the risk of insider threats, improved regulatory compliance, and successfully passed their next audit with minimal security findings.

Another success story involves a healthcare provider that needed to secure access to patient records and critical medical systems. The organization faced challenges with third-party vendors requiring privileged access for system maintenance. Without a structured PAM framework, vendor accounts had long-term access with no expiration, creating a high-security risk. To address this, the healthcare provider implemented just-in-time (JIT) access for vendors, ensuring that privileged credentials were issued only when needed and revoked immediately after use. Additionally, privileged session recording allowed the security team to monitor vendor activities and detect any unauthorized actions. This approach helped prevent unauthorized data access and ensured compliance with HIPAA regulations.

Despite these success stories, many organizations fail to implement PAM effectively, leading to serious security breaches. One such failure occurred in a large retail company that suffered a major data breach due to weak privileged access controls. The breach originated from a compromised third-party vendor account with excessive privileges. Attackers used stolen credentials to access critical databases containing customer payment information. The organization lacked session monitoring and failed to detect the unauthorized access until millions of records had already been exfiltrated. An investigation revealed that the company had no proper access review processes in place, allowing vendor accounts to retain high-level privileges indefinitely. The breach resulted in regulatory fines, reputational damage, and significant financial losses.

A similar failure was observed in a technology company that failed to enforce password rotation for privileged accounts. The company relied on static administrator passwords shared among multiple IT staff members. When a former employee left the organization, they retained knowledge of these credentials and later used them to access internal systems. The lack of PAM controls meant there was no session recording or access logs to track the unauthorized activity. By the time the breach was discovered, the attacker had already deleted sensitive data and disrupted key business operations. This incident highlighted the importance of enforcing automated password rotation, role-based access control (RBAC), and continuous monitoring of privileged activities.

Another case study highlights the risks associated with cloud environments when PAM is not properly extended to cloud workloads. A software company that rapidly migrated its infrastructure to the cloud overlooked the importance of securing cloud-based privileged accounts. Many cloud administrator accounts were created with full access to production environments, but without multi-factor authentication (MFA) or centralized access control. Attackers exploited a misconfigured cloud storage bucket containing sensitive credentials, allowing them to escalate privileges and gain control over the company's cloud resources. The breach led to data leakage and service downtime, forcing the company to reevaluate its PAM strategy and implement stricter cloud access controls.

Organizations that succeed in PAM implementation focus on continuous improvement, regular audits, and integration with broader cybersecurity frameworks. Case studies demonstrate that effective PAM solutions require a combination of least privilege enforcement, real-time monitoring, strong authentication mechanisms, and automated credential management. Failures, on the other hand, often stem from excessive privileges, weak password policies, lack of monitoring, and poor enforcement of access controls.

By learning from both successful and failed PAM implementations, organizations can refine their privileged access strategies and strengthen their overall security posture. Implementing best practices, addressing vulnerabilities, and regularly assessing privileged access policies can help prevent costly breaches and ensure that critical systems remain protected from unauthorized access.

Building a PAM Center of Excellence

Establishing a Privileged Access Management (PAM) Center of Excellence (CoE) is a strategic approach to ensuring long-term security, governance, and operational efficiency in managing privileged accounts. A PAM CoE serves as a centralized framework that drives best practices, continuous improvement, and innovation in privileged access security across an organization. By bringing together expertise, standardized processes, and technology, a CoE enhances the effectiveness of PAM programs, ensuring that privileged access remains secure and compliant with evolving regulations.

One of the foundational steps in building a PAM Center of Excellence is defining its scope and objectives. The CoE should align with the organization's broader security goals, ensuring that privileged access policies support risk reduction, operational resilience, and regulatory compliance. Establishing a clear mission statement helps articulate the CoE's purpose, whether it is focused on minimizing insider threats, enforcing least privilege, or integrating PAM with identity and access management (IAM) frameworks. By setting measurable objectives, organizations can track the effectiveness of their PAM initiatives and adjust strategies as needed.

A dedicated governance structure is critical for a successful PAM CoE. Assigning key roles and responsibilities ensures accountability and effective decision-making. Security leaders, IT administrators, compliance officers, and risk management professionals should collaborate to define policies, assess threats, and drive continuous improvements. Establishing an executive sponsor helps secure leadership support, ensuring that the CoE receives the necessary funding, resources, and organizational backing to operate effectively.

Standardizing PAM processes and policies across the organization helps create consistency in managing privileged access. The CoE should develop enterprise-wide guidelines for privileged account discovery, credential management, access approval workflows, and session monitoring. Documenting these processes in a centralized repository ensures that all teams follow uniform security practices, reducing misconfigurations and compliance risks. Regular policy reviews help adapt PAM controls to new security threats and evolving business needs.

Technology plays a crucial role in enabling a PAM Center of Excellence. Implementing an integrated PAM platform with automated credential vaulting, privileged session monitoring, and real-time analytics enhances security while streamlining operations. The CoE should evaluate and recommend PAM technologies that align with the organization's security architecture, ensuring seamless integration with SIEM, IAM, and endpoint protection systems. Continuous optimization of PAM tools through automation and machine learning enhances threat detection and response capabilities.

Training and awareness programs are essential for fostering a security-first culture within the organization. The CoE should develop structured training programs to educate IT teams, developers, and business users on PAM best practices, threat mitigation strategies, and compliance requirements. Regular workshops, simulations, and phishing awareness campaigns help reinforce the importance of securing privileged access. Establishing a knowledge-sharing platform enables teams to access PAM resources, troubleshooting guides, and policy updates.

Continuous monitoring and metrics-driven evaluation ensure that the PAM CoE remains effective over time. Key performance indicators (KPIs) such as the number of privileged accounts secured, the percentage of automated access requests, and the rate of privilege escalation attempts provide insights into PAM program success. Security teams should conduct periodic audits, risk assessments, and penetration testing to identify vulnerabilities and refine PAM strategies. Integrating PAM analytics with threat intelligence feeds helps detect emerging risks and adapt security controls proactively.

A successful PAM Center of Excellence evolves with the organization's growth and technological advancements. As businesses expand their IT infrastructure to include cloud environments, DevOps workflows, and third-party integrations, the CoE must continuously refine its approach to privileged access security. Leveraging AI-driven threat detection, zero-trust access models, and just-in-time (JIT) privilege provisioning ensures that PAM remains adaptive and resilient against evolving cyber threats.

By centralizing privileged access management expertise, standardizing policies, integrating advanced security technologies, and fostering a culture of continuous improvement, a PAM Center of Excellence strengthens an organization's security posture. It ensures that privileged access is not only protected today but remains secure in the face of future challenges.

Preparing for the Future of PAM

Privileged Access Management (PAM) continues to evolve as organizations adapt to new cybersecurity threats, technological advancements, and regulatory requirements. As cybercriminals develop more sophisticated attack methods, businesses must proactively enhance their PAM strategies to stay ahead of emerging risks. Future-proofing PAM involves leveraging automation, artificial intelligence (AI), Zero Trust principles, and cloud-native security models to ensure that privileged access remains secure in an increasingly complex digital landscape.

The rapid adoption of cloud computing, DevOps, and remote work environments has changed how privileged access is managed. Traditional PAM approaches, which focused on on-premises infrastructure and static privilege assignments, are no longer sufficient in dynamic IT ecosystems. Organizations must transition to cloud-native PAM solutions that support hybrid and multi-cloud environments, ensuring seamless access control across distributed infrastructure. This shift requires integrating PAM with cloud identity providers, enforcing least privilege policies for cloud workloads, and implementing Just-In-Time (JIT) access to minimize persistent administrative privileges.

Artificial intelligence and machine learning (ML) are playing an increasing role in the future of PAM. AI-driven PAM solutions analyze vast amounts of privileged access data to detect anomalies, predict risks, and automate access decisions. Behavioral analytics helps identify deviations from normal privileged user activity, allowing security teams to proactively mitigate potential threats. Instead of relying solely on predefined access policies, AI-enhanced PAM dynamically adjusts privilege levels based on real-time risk assessments, reducing the likelihood of privilege abuse or credential compromise.

Zero Trust security frameworks are becoming integral to PAM strategies. The traditional perimeter-based security model is being replaced by a Zero Trust approach, where no user or system is automatically trusted. Organizations must enforce continuous authentication and verification for all privileged access requests, regardless of whether they originate from within or outside the corporate network. Implementing strong authentication mechanisms such as Multi-Factor Authentication (MFA), biometric verification, and contextual access controls ensures that privileged accounts remain protected against unauthorized access.

The role of machine identities in PAM is expanding as automation and cloud-native architectures become more prevalent. Non-human accounts, such as API keys, service accounts, and containerized workloads, require privileged access to function efficiently. Organizations must extend their PAM frameworks to include machine identity management, ensuring that automated processes adhere to least privilege principles. Secure vaulting, credential rotation, and certificate-based authentication are essential for preventing the misuse of machine identities and reducing the risk of credential-based attacks.

Regulatory compliance requirements are expected to become more stringent in the coming years. Governments and industry bodies are continuously updating data protection and cybersecurity regulations, placing greater emphasis on privileged access controls. Organizations must stay ahead of compliance mandates by implementing audit-ready PAM solutions that provide continuous monitoring, detailed access logs, and automated reporting. Ensuring that PAM frameworks align with standards such as GDPR, HIPAA, PCI DSS, and NIST will help businesses avoid regulatory penalties while strengthening their security posture.

The future of PAM also involves deeper integration with Security Information and Event Management (SIEM) and Security Orchestration, Automation, and Response (SOAR) platforms. By connecting PAM with broader security ecosystems, organizations can enhance threat detection, streamline incident response, and automate remediation efforts. Real-time correlation between privileged access events and security incidents helps security teams identify potential threats faster and take immediate action to contain breaches.

User experience is becoming a key consideration in PAM evolution. Security teams must balance stringent access controls with usability to ensure that privileged users can efficiently perform their tasks without unnecessary friction. Adaptive authentication, role-based access control (RBAC), and frictionless privilege escalation workflows help maintain security while improving user productivity. Future PAM solutions will continue to focus on seamless integration, minimizing disruptions while enforcing strict security controls.

Preparing for the future of PAM requires a proactive approach that embraces automation, AI-driven analytics, Zero Trust principles, and cloud-native security models. Organizations must continuously refine their PAM strategies, adapt to emerging threats, and align with evolving regulatory requirements to protect privileged access effectively. Investing in advanced PAM solutions today will help businesses build a resilient security foundation for the future.

Roadmap to a Comprehensive PAM Program

Implementing a comprehensive Privileged Access Management (PAM) program is essential for securing an organization's critical systems, reducing insider threats, and preventing credential-based cyberattacks. A structured roadmap ensures that privileged access controls are systematically deployed, aligned with security best practices, and capable of evolving with emerging threats. By following a phased approach, organizations can establish a strong foundation for PAM while continuously refining policies, technologies, and processes to enhance privileged access security.

The first step in developing a PAM roadmap is conducting a privileged access assessment. Organizations must identify all privileged accounts, including administrative users, service accounts, application credentials, and machine identities. Many organizations underestimate the number of privileged accounts within their infrastructure, leading to unmanaged risks. A thorough discovery process helps establish visibility into all privileged access points, ensuring that no critical accounts are left unprotected.

Once privileged accounts are identified, organizations must define clear policies and governance frameworks. Establishing a formal PAM policy sets the foundation for enforcing least privilege, implementing role-based access control (RBAC), and defining access approval workflows. Security teams should collaborate with IT administrators, compliance officers, and business stakeholders to ensure that PAM policies align with regulatory requirements, such as GDPR, HIPAA, and PCI DSS.

Deploying a PAM solution requires careful planning and integration with existing security infrastructure. Organizations should implement a centralized credential vault to store and manage privileged credentials securely. Automated password rotation ensures that privileged accounts do not use static credentials, reducing the risk of credential compromise. Multi-factor authentication (MFA) should be enforced for all privileged access, ensuring that unauthorized users cannot exploit stolen credentials.

Privileged session management is a critical component of a comprehensive PAM program. Organizations must monitor and record privileged activities to detect unauthorized actions and ensure compliance with security policies. Session recording, keystroke logging, and real-time analytics help security teams identify potential threats and respond to suspicious behavior. Integrating PAM with Security Information and Event Management (SIEM) solutions enhances threat detection and incident response capabilities.

As organizations expand their IT environments, PAM strategies must scale accordingly. Implementing Just-In-Time (JIT) access provisioning minimizes standing privileges, ensuring that elevated access is granted only when necessary and revoked automatically after use. Extending PAM controls to cloud platforms, containerized workloads, and third-party vendors helps secure privileged access across hybrid and multi-cloud environments.

Continuous improvement is key to maintaining an effective PAM program. Organizations should conduct regular privilege audits, access reviews, and security assessments to identify gaps and refine PAM policies. User training and awareness programs ensure that IT administrators, developers, and employees understand privileged access risks and follow security best practices.

A well-defined roadmap provides a structured approach to deploying, scaling, and optimizing PAM, ensuring that privileged access remains secure while supporting business operations. By focusing on discovery, policy development, technology implementation, monitoring, and continuous improvement, organizations can build a resilient PAM program that effectively mitigates security risks.

Conclusion and Final Thoughts

Privileged Access Management (PAM) has become an essential component of modern cybersecurity strategies, protecting organizations from the ever-growing risks associated with privileged accounts. As businesses continue to expand their digital footprints, the need for robust PAM solutions becomes increasingly critical. The management of privileged access is no longer just a technical concern but a fundamental aspect of risk management, compliance, and overall cybersecurity resilience. Organizations that fail to implement effective PAM controls expose themselves to credential theft, insider threats, and regulatory non-compliance, all of which can have severe financial and reputational consequences.

Securing privileged access requires a multi-layered approach that includes least privilege enforcement, strong authentication mechanisms, continuous monitoring, and automated credential management. PAM solutions provide organizations with the tools necessary to protect sensitive assets, control administrative access, and detect potential security incidents in real time. By integrating PAM with broader security frameworks such as Zero Trust, Identity and Access Management (IAM), and Security Information and Event Management (SIEM), organizations can establish a comprehensive defense strategy that minimizes attack surfaces and enhances threat detection.

The role of automation and artificial intelligence in PAM continues to grow, offering new ways to streamline privileged access controls and improve security posture. Machine learning algorithms can analyze access behaviors to detect anomalies, while automated workflows can enforce just-in-time (JIT) access, reducing the risk of standing privileges. As cyber threats become more sophisticated, leveraging AI-driven analytics within PAM frameworks will help organizations proactively mitigate risks before they escalate into full-scale breaches.

Compliance and regulatory requirements also drive the need for robust PAM implementation. Frameworks such as GDPR, HIPAA, PCI DSS, and NIST mandate strict access controls, audit logging, and privileged session monitoring. Organizations must continuously assess their privileged access policies to ensure compliance and adapt to evolving regulatory landscapes. A well-implemented PAM program not only strengthens security but also simplifies audit processes and demonstrates due diligence in protecting sensitive data.

Implementing PAM is not a one-time effort but an ongoing journey that requires continuous refinement and adaptation to emerging threats. Organizations must regularly review access controls, conduct privilege audits, and provide security training to employees. A strong PAM strategy is built on a culture of security awareness, where users understand the risks associated with privileged accounts and follow best practices to safeguard credentials.

The future of PAM lies in its ability to evolve alongside technological advancements and shifting threat landscapes. Cloud-native PAM solutions, Zero Trust security models, and AI-driven analytics will continue to shape how organizations manage privileged access. Investing in PAM today ensures that businesses remain resilient against cyber threats while maintaining operational efficiency and compliance with industry regulations.

Organizations that take a proactive approach to PAM implementation will not only strengthen their security posture but also gain a competitive advantage by demonstrating their commitment to protecting sensitive information. By embracing best practices, leveraging advanced technologies, and fostering a security-first culture, businesses can effectively manage privileged access and reduce the risk of security breaches. The ongoing development of PAM strategies will remain a priority for organizations seeking to secure their most valuable assets in an increasingly complex digital world.